SARDINIAN CHRONICLES

SARDINIAN

CHRONICLES

Bernard Lortat-Jacob

Foreword by Michel Leiris

Translated by Teresa Lavender Fagan

THE UNIVERSITY OF CHICAGO PRESS
Chicago and London

R

the Centre National de la Recherche
ng in Mediterranean music, he directs the
e de l'Homme.

THE UNIVERSITY OF CHICAGO PRESS, CHICAGO 60637
THE UNIVERSITY OF CHICAGO PRESS, LTD., LONDON

© 1995 by The University of Chicago
All rights reserved. Published 1995

Printed in the United States of America

03 02 01 00 99 98 97 96 95   1 2 3 4 5

ISBN: 0-226-49340-7 (cloth)
ISBN: 0-226-49341-5 (paper)

Originally published in Paris as *Chroniques sardes,* © Julliard 1990.

LIBRARY OF CONGRESS CATALOGING-IN-PUBLICATION DATA

Lortat-Jacob, Bernard.
    [Chroniques sardes.   English]
    Sardinian chronicles / Bernard Lortat-Jacob; foreword by Michel
Leiris; translated by Teresa Lavender Fagan.
        p.   cm. — (Chicago studies in ethnomusicology)
    Includes bibliographical references and index.
    1. Sardinia (Italy—Social life and customs. 2. Accordionists—
Italy—Sardinia—Social life and customs. I. Title. II. Series.
DG975.S33L6713   1995
945.9—dc20   94-10766
                                                                        CIP

⊗ The paper used in this publication meets the minimum requirements of the American
National Standard for Information Sciences—Permanence of Paper for Printed Library
Materials, ANSI Z39.48-1984.

To Maria

CONTENTS

FOREWORD

LIKE KARL MARX WHO, AS HE PUT IT, GAVE NEW LIFE TO
HEGEL'S DIALECTICS, BERNARD LORTAT-JACOB IS ONE OF THOSE
RESEARCHERS WHO TEND, WHETHER THEY MEAN TO OR NOT, TO
BRING ETHNOGRAPHY BACK TO LIFE. PORTRAYING LIVING PEOPLE AND
THEIR BEHAVIOR RATHER THAN FOCUSING PRIMARILY ON THEIR INSTITU-
TIONS, EXAMINING THE TECHNIQUES THEY BRING INTO PLAY AND THEIR
WAYS OF SEEING THE WORLD, AS WELL AS ALL THE MATERIAL SIGNS OF
THEIR EXISTENCE: IS THIS NOT THE TRULY HUMAN GOAL OF A SCIENCE
THAT IS TOO OFTEN DIVERTED FROM THE CONCRETE, TOWARD JARGON-
ISTIC ABSTRACTIONS?

From patron saint fête to patron saint fête, from musician to musician
(usually accordionists), shown practicing their profession as well as in
their homes, with their individual habits and circle of friends, we are introduced not simply to the music of the residents of rural Sardinia but also
to the customs of those inhabiting that island. It is a place that Bernard
Lortat-Jacob, a musicologist but also himself a practicing amateur accordionist, has traveled with love and patience. In the series of brief vignettes
he shares with us, his interactions with all those—musicians and others—
whom he needed for his study appear as adventures, quite different from
the somewhat disembodied shape assumed by most ethnographers'
working relationships with those referred to in the business as "infor-
mants," as if they were assistants in a police investigation.

Flesh-and-blood characters—the men and women Bernard Lortat-
Jacob encountered in the course of his fieldwork—are described in their
every vital dimension, and we learn in the most direct of ways from the
portraits of these people as much about their unique personalities as we
do about the characteristics of the social milieu in which they live. Eager
to provide comprehensive accounts, the author willingly includes himself
in his portraits along with his hopes, disappointments, and weariness, but

above all his complete unconditional affection for the men and women whose likeness he sketches; yet he is quick to criticize when he sees fit to do so.

A gallery of living portraits—this is how one might define Bernard Lortat-Jacob's work, a work that makes the lay reader sense that there do indeed exist human beings called "Sardinians," and does so with far more success than would a study that hid them behind a rather weighty description of their intellectual systems, their ways and customs, or their environment.

—*Michel Leiris*

THE FERRY

In the port of Genoa amidst the ferries from la Tirrenia, the greatest confusion reigns. The wide esplanade leading to the ships leaving for Sardinia is always full of people. If a strike should happen to complicate matters, the port then resembles a nomads' camping ground. People sleep in their cars, waiting for the next boat to leave in the morning. Rumors circulate, as if wantonly aggravating the situation, while the *panini* sold at the little portside stand double in price. There is no more room on the boat. The arguments of travelers pleading for a speedy departure revolve around tragedies in which a woman is always at center stage: a sick daughter, a pregnant wife, or a dying grandmother. My wife, Maria, who in an attempt to join me the year before had chosen the latter argument to get on board, received this reply: "*Figuratevi, signorina, quante nonne sono malate in questo periodo!*" "If you only knew, *signorina*, how many grandmothers are sick at this time of the year!"

On board, the crew of the *Clodia* must choose among several strategies when rejecting requests for sleeping rooms. Depending on who the travelers are and the number of times they've made the crossing, crew members either resort to a few set excuses indicating their exasperation or else they show courtesy: their lack of power then serves as an argument.

A big handwritten sign is permanently posted announcing that there are no more seats available on the boat. From the curtness of its tone alone the sign is suspicious. In Italian collective affairs that lead to a dead end

1

the normal reaction is to try to circumvent the problem. All in good form. And form is essentially oral. In Mediterranean countries things seem to acquire a reality only when they are debated out loud: The supremacy of the written word is only apparent. Considered unreliable, what is written down is always subject to discussion.

In any event, the ferry is the world of the spoken word, where the Neapolitan dialect of the crew members, the polished Italian of those who wish to pass for *signori*, and the Sardinian of those returning to their own country all intersect.

On board there are always a few Sardinian grandmothers in long skirts, fixed and immobile, huddled up against a side of the ship, and one or two souls traveling alone who invariably fall to my lot during each of my crossings.

This time it was Cocco. Cocco Sannu. I had noticed him because he was so short, and because of his weatherbeaten face and his cap. He traveled regularly, often going back and forth between Sardinia where he lived and the continent where his family had emigrated.

On board he had his little habits. Unlike most of the passengers who, once the hubbub of the first hour had passed, quickly found themselves a little spot in which nervously to await their arrival, Cocco approached his journey with the assurance of a petty officer. He moved freely around the entire boat totally at ease, as if he were a permanent resident, and spent the entire night awake. He never missed a film being shown, spent some spare change in the noisy canteen, and knew the names of the waiters in the various bars.

But above all he spent long hours on deck studying the sky.

He invited me to join him.

Examining the sky is both the starting point and the culmination of every spiritual quest, so that the inventory of planets can never be done without personal involvement; before Cocco was able to determine the time it took to get to Saturn and Jupiter, we were already there.

The sky arranged itself before my eyes like a familiar space. Animal shapes, revealed in the different constellations, were recalled, prolonged, and redrawn. For the Dog, the Serpent, Aquila the Eagle, the Bull, the Ram, and the two Bears Cocco invented expressions or attitudes derived from his knowledge of nature: the Serpent has two shining eyes, the Dog, with an open mouth, is ready to eat Castor and Pollux, Aquila and the Ram fear and respect each other, and that is why much of the sky separates them. But from the large white boat where we stood nothing separated Cocco from a sky he embraced in all its familiar breadth.

o

Cocco had a trade: he raised chickens. At first I thought chickens were part of his astronomic observations and I attributed the introduction of domestic fowl into the conversation to the mediocrity of my Italian: I must have missed a link in the conversational chain. But when the theme was taken up again I realized I was wrong. He was talking about real chickens and not constellations in the shape of those animals.

We were now settled in the bar. Using a pencil, Cocco scribbled on paper napkins and drew a map of the sky and the layout of his henhouses in such a way that they appeared almost identical. Everything had been placed just so for the contentment of the creatures inhabiting his farmyard. He had some "French" chickens from Houdan, I think (this was supposed to be of interest to me), which unfortunately were much too fragile. He had built a special shelter for them next to his house. The *Cocincine* (Cochin-China fowl, I gather) had strong personalities and had to be stimulated for a long time before they would lay their eggs.

The layout of the farmyard was taking shape. Each building was a different color, built of certain materials, and had different technical devices which were used to dispense a balanced diet to the chickens. This system went beyond Cocco's farmyard into a network of relationships he had in the village. Five or six people were involved regularly to insure the proper functioning of the chicken yard: a fisherman friend brought tiny sea creatures that were ground up in a machine (they were good for eggs); and his brother-in-law obtained food for him at a good price. As for Cocco himself, he was able several times a year to glean on the rich plains of the Campidano. He was also acquainted with the manager of a canteen and was the close friend of a neighbor woman who owned a large farm. They took turns providing supplies for his little factory.

This communal system provided a practical response to technical de-

3

mands. It extended Cocco's initiatives while taking advantage of the rational nature of the whole.

o

Cocco studied the sky as a peasant and organized his hen houses as a geometrician, indeed as a meticulous astronomer. Reversing the order of realities, he observed familiar creatures in celestial infinity and conducted his affairs with a sense of the coordination unique to things of the universe.

He put so much passion into his descriptions and so much conviction into his enterprise that I wondered whether he didn't intervene directly in the production of eggs. I don't really remember how he induced his *Cocincine* to lay; I imagined him crouched on his short legs mimicking the laying position . . .

o

I had attempted several times to direct the conversation to my own obsessions and to the goal of my trip, inviting him to talk about music.

Musical instruments alone whetted his aesthetic appetite. He understood how they worked and knew the traditions of his village. Living in a land of reeds and canes he had once built *trumbittas* for his young nephews—very simple clarinets whose sound could be amplified using hollowed-out gourds. In his youth he had also fashioned the *serragia* that was played during Carnival—a sort of caricature of the cello whose bow was made out of a few stretched horsehairs and whose sound box was a pig's bladder stuck on top of a broomstick. He also told me about a prehistoric instrument made out of resonant stones arranged as drums and played like a marimba.

But in truth music was not Cocco's forte. He placed a greater value on poetry and repeated what I had already heard from a barber in Orgosolo who was a poetry enthusiast: "One can't love both music and poetry at the same time!" A strange assertion, quite different from the usual beliefs, which easily associate meaning and form, the "spoken" and the "sung." But with the blunt position he held Cocco demonstrated his innate ability

Listening to a poetry joust (*gara poetica*). Tonara (1979).
Photo by Bernard Lortat-Jacob.

to create systems out of nuances. A unitary principle led him to turn the
sky into the object of a taxonomy based on the shapes of animals, and to
make his henhouses the center of the universe. The distinction he made
between sung poetry and music was part of this same obsession for classi-
fication. The fact that in Sardinia poetry *is* sung made little difference.

I initiated a discussion with Cocco on the subject of that opposition worthy to serve as a theme for Sardinian poets themselves when they square off on village squares in long extemporaneous contests.

o

Cocco believed that music, unlike poetry, did not fall within the domain of the spirit. Granted, it could be beautiful, but it was meant above all to please dancers. Cocco didn't like the pleasures of the flesh, scorning everything that more or less escaped his empirical calculations. I had to argue for a long time before allowing him to go off once again into the realms in which he excelled: the realms of experimental technology and inspired tinkering.

On the ferry's deck the sea breeze brought thoughts that were made clearer by repeated trips to the bar. The night passed in this way, until the first stars disappeared into the dawn.

With daybreak came the gradual appearance of the island of Asinara, and one could just barely make out the Stintino peninsula. In the rush to disembark I lost sight of Cocco after having seen him one last time leaning up against two enormous suitcases each held together with strings.

o

The sleepless night began to weigh on me. I thought of Cocco who would have to endure an entire day under the hot July sun in a train and a bus to reach his village and henhouses.

In any event, our paths did diverge. My relationship with nature was that of a city dweller and the one I had with technology was vague: I had never even been curious enough to open up the sophisticated tape recorder I used in my work to observe its internal mechanism. I headed for the first bar to organize my trip with a glass of wine in front of me.

DESULO

ONCE YOU GET PAST FONNI AND ITS PHALLIC BELLTOWER (THE HIGHEST PERCHED IN ALL SARDINIA, WITH EXACT EQUIVALENTS IN PROVENCE AND DOBROGEA), THE ROAD PLUNGES INTERMINABLY IN ORDER TO CROSS A TRIBUTARY OF THE TIRSU RIVER, A THIN TRICKLE OUT OF ALL PROPORTION WITH THE DETOUR IT IMPOSES. THE ROAD THEN CLIMBS ON UP TOWARD TONARA.

Tonara was in the midst of a fête, judging from the large number of cars and the accordion music being piped through loudspeakers.

Totore Pichiaddas was alone at the front of a small stage. Like the stage itself he would be stuck there on the square for three days. He was playing a small accordion with eight basses whose case he had wrapped in a yellow, slightly spangled covering. On one side the little stage hung over the deep valley, and on the other it overlooked the square (where not many people were around yet). It faced a still empty space, turning its back on a landscape that disappeared into the afternoon mist.

With his legs spread apart, Pichiaddas was solidly seated on a chair. In his voluminous shorts, which rode high up on his legs, his rubber thongs, and his loosely knit T-shirt, he didn't cut a very elegant figure. But his stature was impressive. Portly and wider than he was tall, he played with a self-confidence proportionate to his size. His accordion was part of his body; it was a natural extension of his hands, which, because of his girth, did not seem to be able to meet in front of his belly. When he played his gestures appeared to be quite ordinary—less expansive than those used in a normal conversation: his arms barely moved, his body never swayed, and the solidity of the whole rested entirely on the symmetry of his movements. Locked in a constant rhythm, he played ever-changing melodic formulas, at once original and familiar. A boy served as his assistant, proud to be helping: he was holding the microphone until the festival committee could unearth a suitable stand for it. The square was left completely to the village children. The sound system was the coveted toy they were all fiddling with. The scaffolding of the little podium, made up of intersecting metallic tubes, was used for gymnastic feats: the stage was a perfect springboard for jumping. The pervading presence of children did not bode well. Spontaneous as it may have appeared, they were not there by chance. At rural fêtes in Europe their presence means the adults have given up: children take over the festivities or rites their elders no longer believe in; they fill a gap and, what is more, they bear witness to a post abandoned. Pichiaddas, all the while continuing to play, chased the kids who were getting too close to his car (a brand new Fiat 127 parked below), talked with men from the festival committee who had come to see

A musician and children on the *palco*. Tonara (1979).
Photo by Bernard Lortat-Jacob.

him, greeted a friend he hadn't seen for a few days, and, as I walked up and introduced myself, talked to me about Sardinian music.

During these moments of distracted attention his playing changed to less acrobatic melodic formulas, while the rhythm, as if permanently fixed, lost none of its assurance: the sound was full, and the beauty of his playing lay in his artful transitions; the beats were strictly marked, but it was inside them that things really happened. The whole was bound together and was as voluble as a conversation that nothing can disturb. Pichiaddas finally stopped playing, and replaced himself with a cassette recording made while he was playing. He put the tape recorder on the chair in his place. His presence had been extended; he was now calm and available; his music continued. We drank a glass of wine. The time was not right for conversation (truth to tell, with him it never really was), and we arranged a meeting for the next day at his house in Desulo.

The fête, in the strict sense of the term, "got rolling" in the late afternoon. The children then had twice as much energy; they invaded the premises, trying out sketchy dance steps alongside the young men and a few young women who were dancing in small groups. The old people would come later in the evening, at nightfall.

The dance gradually curved into an arc, from which a few young couples broke off. Pichiaddas's playing became more animated, marked by the brilliant style of Desulo. The Tonara people lost themselves in these spiraling progressions. Then the pace picked up a little. This was not too much of a problem for the dancers in the circle who, swaying slowly side to side, were satisfied with simply marking the beats of the dance. On the other hand, the couples who had left the circle had trouble adjusting their improvised steps. As they danced by the stage they hurled abuse at the musician leading them. As for him, he only seemed to enjoy provoking the dancers and became increasingly daring. He ignored their shouts. Shrugging his shoulders without raising his tone, he grumbled, just to show he understood what they were asking, while his playing grew even more frenzied. For a musician, playing for a dance involves satisfying the dancers and comes down to listening to their requests. That those requests might be varied and contradictory does not change matters. Two series of steps alternate regularly: the calmly measured *passu bassu,* which is performed

9

Ballu in piazza (dance in the village square). Irgoli (1993).
Photo by Bernard Lortat-Jacob.

flush to the ground in a lateral movement, and the *passu altu,* which
sometimes occasions quite acrobatic jumping.

o

Whereas the older people elegantly strut along with a most perfect
economy of movement, the young dancers always enjoy leaping about
and especially love the *passu altu,* which enables them to show off their
youthful vigor.

The entire art of the musician resides in his choice of musical formulas
that, depending on their configurations, call for either smooth gliding or
unbridled leaping. Too much jumping would exhaust the dancers; but if
there isn't enough, the dance would be boring. Pichiaddas, an expert in
this matter, has found the perfect solution: His art is based on expectation. He is the architect of that expectation, and into his most strictly for-

Ballu in piazza (dance in the village square)—detail. Irgoli (1993).
Photo by Bernard Lortat-Jacob.

mulaic cadences he introduces a few accents that make the dancers think
that the *passu altu* will not be long in coming: the anticipation of frenzy is
perhaps greater than the frenzy itself.

Sometimes, on hearing those accents the young dancers leap before it
is really time to do so. The older folk let it happen; their feet still retain all
their mobility, but their jumps, just barely indicated by a straightening of
their bodies, are only hints of jumps, just as their dancing is a sketch of the
dance steps.

o

The square was now full and the stage teeming with bodies: people
were drinking on it, walking on it, pausing for a moment on it; in between
two dances someone came to announce that some car keys had been lost.
Children insisted on being allowed to make the announcements. All were
acceptable provided they were of concern to someone and were made in
Italian. At the microphone—and at the microphone alone—Italian dom-

inated. One also heard the lyrical flights of an improvised commentator orating excitedly because with the wine he had drunk he could no longer keep his convivial excitement to himself.

Pichiaddas now started a waltz that a vacationing couple from the city had requested, a specifically Sardinian version of the waltz: every beat is marked with equal intensity. Bodies are meant to be held stiff and it is impossible for dancers to allow themselves any expressive *rubatos*. One can easily imagine how revolutionary the introduction of the waltz that required couples to hold one another must have been in Sardinia. Here, following the style called *liscio* (literally, "the smooth"), the waltz is danced face to face. Dancers look at each other without ever touching. As for their arms, they never embrace; they are used to keep bodies at a distance, not to bring them closer together. Dancers glide along. Virtuosity resides in the art of covering a lot of ground. Two or three well-matched couples held everyone's attention.

Night gradually brought some calm to the square. There were fewer announcements at the microphone and the *ballu tundu* (the "round dance") was now formed. Apparently no one else lost his keys, and Pichiaddas played dances one after the other without interruption.

Small bars, set up for the occasion on the edge of the square, were noisy rest stops, constantly filled with people. Rounds of drinks grew more numerous as did the obligation to consume.

Late in the night, as the fête was drawing to a close, there was no question of lingering: some act of mischief almost naturally prolonging everyone's excitement was always possible. Alongside Pichiaddas, though, I was not too fearful. Even more than his bulk, his uniqueness protected me: he was the soul of the fête.

While he was getting ready to pack up, the young members of the festival committee played around with his accordion. They managed a few passable notes, stressing how difficult the instrument was to play by their expressive frowns—no doubt to point out how far off the mark they were and, at the same time, to pay homage to the best musician in the region.

Pichiaddas listened to them absentmindedly without giving them any advice. He was not obliged to, and anyway, there was no method for attaining the knowledge he had. Nothing was more foreign to him than pedagogy. He took his instrument back for a moment, just to show how he did it—thus how it should be done: he played as usual; there was no question of his going into detail. In any case, there was only one way of playing—his.

o

In the course of my work I often suffered from Pichiaddas's unpedagogic practices. Any discussion of music and its techniques was immediately hurried over: with a burst of words Pichiaddas would grab his accordion to illustrate everything and nothing. Simply for the pleasure of playing. It was particularly difficult to find an illustration of anything in his playing.

At the time I had one preoccupation: I wanted to discover what was inherited and what was acquired in Pichiaddas's fundamentally imaginative music, and on what real foundation he had built his astonishing sets of variations; who had been his master; and finally, how he had built up his repertoire.

I had asked these questions of various musicians any number of times, but their answers were always obscure. Dance tunes did not really have authors: older musicians (most often fathers) played more slowly, always the same dance, without ever bringing in the slightest variation. The music became more complicated on its own through the generations, without anyone knowing quite how it happened.

Anyhow, the problem was less a matter of knowing the origin of such enrichment than of knowing whom it benefited. In fact, it benefits everyone, for as soon as they are invented by a musician and put into circulation from village square to village square, new variations become common property, or, more precisely, communal property, for dances belong to a collective, village system: if it is heard, understood, and memorized, the musical work of one musician naturally becomes the property of all.

With the aim of enriching his playing, of enlarging his repertoire, and also of increasing his chances of being hired to play at fêtes, Pichiaddas, like all professional musicians, worked alone, at night, in his kitchen and went over his repertoire the way a stamp collector reviews his entire collection to savor its richness. In the meager space allotted to possible innovations he added variations of his own to the traditional stock he had inherited. He naturally borrowed some of them; but when he was responsible for providing a musical accompaniment, he was of course incapable of differentiating between his own variations and those of others.

Owing to intense rivalries between musicians, borrowing is easily viewed as theft. The entire problem, for Pichiaddas as for his colleagues, lay in the always conflictual appropriation of stolen musical assets. Failing at least in part in this delicate transfer of property, Pichiaddas was subject, as were others, to attack from his rivals. He was thus accused of theft, even of pillage. By whom, namely? By Salvatore Dillu.

o

I got involved in the quarrel and the next day, taken discreetly by one of the cabal's participants, I went and saw Dillu.

I had already learned a lot about him—his moodiness and distrust would make my visit difficult.

Dillu had retired from competition several years earlier. For personal reasons he no longer played. He had left the square, and had abandoned all his work to the memory of those for whom he had played. Later on he conceived the idea of selling his repertoire. According to him, whoever stepped forward to buy it would be able to play what he used to play. The asking price: two million lire.

I went to his house specifically to discuss his offer. His children seemed surprised at my visit and informed me that he was working on the roof of one of the houses being built in a neighboring area (like many accordionists, he was also a mason).

But all, or almost all, of the houses in Desulo were under construction. Even more than in other villages in Sardinia. Desulo was a huge work site where it was difficult to find a house that had been completed.

I got lost in the narrow streets and dead ends on my way to see him. Like all villages in Sardinia, Desulo had inherited three types of architecture: heavy foundations of unfinished buildings, the exclusive realm of rough perpends and bare brick; old houses that henceforth assume the landscape's rugged forms and whose stones, taken from the very site on which the houses are built, reflect the color of the land; and finally, the Old Ones, which constitute perhaps the only true architecture of the country: these buildings always seem to go together in perfect harmony, and, appearing more solidly fixed than the constructions around them, they have been sitting in the same places for centuries.

I finally flushed out Dillu, who was hard at work over a cement mixer. From what I told him, or rather from what my somewhat awkward companions told him, he understood that I was a rich foreigner who had finally come to realize his dreams. I was the buyer he had been waiting for.

We ended up discussing money before we discussed music. Two million? Why this sum, and what for? But this was a matter that had to be discussed calmly; besides, the cement mixer was turning. We made plans to meet that evening at his house.

o

Salvatore had prepared himself for this meeting, which was held in the cellar of his house. He had put on a dark suit—his Sunday best—and a tie. He seemed to have understood that his offer had to be justified. What in fact was he selling? The village dance? The old people's dance? The dance that belonged to everyone? Who was swindling whom in these circumstances, and how could he justify being the sole beneficiary in a transaction whose rules he was arbitrarily setting?

He restated and commented on his proposition in an obsessive way, for a subject can only be seen as important if it is repeated: in the dance of Desulo, everything came from him, "except the dancers' steps." I wanted to let him talk, but my companions intervened. Their indignation was frank: that music was not written down, it had no author; it belonged to everyone and had existed forever. Therefore it could not be sold.

Salvatore assumed an attitude of detachment that seemed natural to him; he let the others speak while appearing to be holding some logic in reserve. He replied, "When he passes on his practice, doesn't a doctor ask for money from his successor?" At least that's what he'd been led to believe. He'd heard it from a learned friend, a *professore*. And didn't he, Salvatore, possess a knowledge equivalent to that of a doctor? Wasn't he passing on to whoever wanted to pay the price for his music the squares and the fêtes to which he had been invited, just as a doctor passes on his practice? If he hadn't been there after the war, when Sardinian music was in such bad shape, music, like his doctor friend's patients, would be dead in Desulo. It was thanks to him, he said, that dance music and the very soul of Sardinia had not vanished from the country.

In this battle of arguments, however, a link was missing; all was not said. Why this forced sale? Why had he left the profession when his visible, pervasive passion for music was obviously still present? I had happened to learn from his neighbors that he sometimes played in the evening at home, but alone and only for himself.

Apparently things could not be said in a hurry. The men who had accompanied me probably gave rise to a certain uneasiness. So we talked about something else to make it appear that everything had been said on the subject, and I discreetly set up another meeting with him for the next day. I would go alone. In addition I wanted to record his priceless musical variations. But nothing could be less certain.

o

The next day I went into his house, which distinguished itself by the degree of disorder that reigned inside. Salvatore, who never had guests, apologized for it. Two or three children scampered around in the shadows. Their father spoke to them harshly. The disorder seemed to be the result of several years of neglect.

In any event, the condition of the premises called for some explanation, and the latter was not long in coming. Salvatore Dillu had lost his wife seven years earlier. He didn't speak of her as a wife, but as a young and beautiful lover; a photo, decorated with wilted flowers, backed this up. In Sardinian family photos the eyes of the deceased are always burning. The subjects must stare into the lens with enough intensity to last for eternity.

The neglect, the decline, and ultimately the entire biography of Salvatore Dillu were all linked by the violence of that death. In fact, it was after the death of his wife that he had stopped playing, in every sense of the word. He had not withdrawn from the village square for a conventional reason, for simple mourning, which traditionally required musicians to stop playing for a month; but quite simply because he could no longer

16

play a note. It was later, when forced by necessity, that he had decided to sell his repertoire in order at least "not to lose everything," he said, and to hear no more about it.

I understood that his decision was not based on monetary interests. For him it was quite simply a matter of burying, along with his wife, all his joys forever. The fact that his proposal was not an admissible one (and had, moreover, never encountered anything but amused curiosity) did not concern him. He wanted to signify an end. However, no one wanted to sign the deed.

o

I brought Salvatore my accordion. This instrument, which was quite beautiful and of a make unknown in Sardinia, sparked the interest of all musicians. It was in fact irresistible and I still remember that, the year before, Francesco Cambiadas, an accordionist from Oliena, wanted to trade me his car for it. Believing my refusal came from an underestimation of his car, and to induce me to accept his offer, he added various objects to balance things out: notably a silver chandelier, which was not really beautiful but was supposed to derive its value from its unusual style. In fact, it had come from a church.

Salvatore contemplated the instrument for a long time before attempting to get a sound out of it. The situation in which he had put himself, and the very price of what he wanted to sell, made any sidestepping impossible. It seemed to me that we had already talked a lot, but he took even more time to discuss things at length. His style of playing, he said, was inimitable. I argued perniciously that from that fact alone it was unsellable, for how could you buy something that was impossible to reproduce? And if it was inimitable, how could he accuse others of having stolen it?

The argument ended up in a flow of nuances and evasions in which I was lost. But the heart of the problem was that, for the first time in seven years, Dillu had to play in front of someone. He was afraid, though playing in front of a foreigner was of less consequence. But the exercise was hard; he had at the same time to rediscover the notes and to go back in time. At first he simply sketched musical phrases instead of really playing them, as if he were clearing out the cobwebs of his memory. In fact, his hand

17

didn't follow. He stopped every thirty seconds to complain of discomfort, which also served to justify his deficiencies. First he played the brief prelude with which every instrumentalist signs his style, then gradually entered into the music by starting with the sequences he visibly cherished. But as if they didn't have enough meaning in themselves, he credited each one with a set of metaphors. Colors, forms, odors, and all his memories intersected in networks that became increasingly dense, gradually drawing closer the image of the one whom it was no longer necessary to evoke, so strong was her presence. Section by section he reconstructed his dance, without, however, ever giving an idea of it as a whole.

Little by little I discovered that Dillu possessed the genius of all great improvisers. He must undoubtedly have played like no one else, but it was unlikely that he would ever again play as he once had. Only exceptional conditions brought him the things he needed to say and the notes he needed to play. I counted for very little in all of this.

During the time when he gave life to the square for dancing and when all Desulo followed him, he remembered that at the end of an evening he was incapable of knowing what he had really played. While playing, his fingers moved along with crazy speed; they literally inhabited the instrument. As if, beyond his control, they went beyond the keyboard, beyond familiar paths.

He spent the short night that followed a performance trying to call to mind his musical adventures of the evening, but was never able to do so. His musical lucidity disappeared outside the playing itself. He lived his experience as a musician with an intensity that I've never observed in anyone else—except perhaps Glenn Gould.

I asked him if I might record his playing. He refused, no doubt because he couldn't trust a foreigner so quickly, but above all because nothing he played would ever be satisfactory. In a way his refusal was a relief: my request was inopportune and quite inappropriate to the business at hand. In any case, I didn't really see how a machine that captures sound while ignoring the conditions in which it is produced could have a place here.

When it came time to leave, Dillu asked me to let him borrow my accordion for a day or two. I would have to stay longer than planned in Desulo, but I agreed; I became an accomplice.

o

Although it wasn't easy to spy on him, I think he played, closed up in his room, for two days without stopping. He made himself scarce—I believe I understand why—when I came to get my accordion on the second day. The first time I went he wasn't home. The second time one of his sons took me to a neighbor's house. I found my accordion there, placed in its box, without comment or an accompanying note.

I never saw Salvatore Dillu again; he didn't answer my letters and I don't even know if he's still alive.

o

Before leaving Desulo I owed one last visit to Totore Pichiaddas, Dillu's fortunate rival. It was difficult to finesse my way out of explaining the two days I had spent with Dillu.

I wasn't expecting any kind words concerning someone who was considered an eccentric. I was, however, surprised to find that Pichiaddas spoke somewhat considerately of the man whose place he had taken. At least he didn't heap insults upon him, which is something in itself.

Pichiaddas was silent with regard to my escapades. It was clear that for him music belonged to the one who was playing it. As for the dance of Desulo, he sold it every night, he said, when he was invited *in piazza* and was paid for playing. That's all he asked. In any event, he could barely manage alone to meet the demand for his playing, so numerous were the requests. I've heard this assertion from almost every musician I've talked to. They all claim to be too much in demand when, for most of them, nothing is further from the truth. They assert as much quite simply in order for it to be so.

Pichiaddas put the entire weight of his large body into this declaration: there could be no doubt that the number of requests for his services was a good indication of his talent; but above all those requests justified his rights of preception: under his name alone, which overshadowed musicians in mourning and those beaten down by the passing of time, Desulo, its dance, and its music were one.

OLIENA

FRANCESCO CAMBIADAS WAS AN AC-
CORDIONIST IN A VILLAGE THAT HAD
MANY: OLIENA. BUT HE WAS THE MOST
FAMOUS OF THEM ALL, AND WAS KNOWN
THROUGHOUT ALL BARBAGIA. HE WAS AWARE
OF HIS FAME AND, WHAT IS MORE, KNEW HOW
TO MAINTAIN IT. HE WAS BENEVOLENTLY CON-
DESCENDING TOWARD HIS YOUNGER COLLEAGUES, AND FLATTERY,
ALONG WITH HIS ACCORDION, WAS OBVIOUSLY THE WEAPON HE WIELDED
MOST ABLY. HIS FLATTERY WAS NOT INNOCENT. ITS GOAL WAS TO NEU-
TRALIZE THE YOUNGEST MUSICIANS WHO ASPIRED TO A FAME EQUAL TO
HIS OWN. BY EMPHATICALLY COMPLIMENTING THE MOST MEDIOCRE
ONES, CAMBIADAS LED THEM TO BELIEVE THEY WERE HIS EQUALS. IN
FACT, HE EXPECTED THAT SAME MEDIOCRITY TO COMMUNICATE THE OP-
POSITE MESSAGE. SO IT WAS THAT AT FÊTES WHERE HE WAS INVITED TO
PLAY BUT THAT HE COULD NOT ATTEND OWING TO AN OVERABUNDANCE
OF WORK, HE ALWAYS HEARTILY RECOMMENDED A SECOND-RATE MUSI-
CIAN TO TAKE HIS PLACE. HE BENEFITED DIRECTLY FROM THIS PRACTICE
BECAUSE WHEN PEOPLE HEARD A DISAPPOINTING PERFORMANCE, THEY
WERE SURE TO POINT OUT WOEFULLY THE ABSENCE OF THE MASTER. WHEN
IT CAME TO DANCE AND ACCORDION MUSIC, FRANCESCO CAMBIADAS HAD
THE BEARING OF A SKILLFUL SEIGNEUR WHOSE MEASURE COULD BE TAKEN
BY THE UNMEASURED COMPLIMENTS HE PAID TO OTHERS.

As for myself, what I liked about Cambiadas was his elegance: he sketched, embellished, and emphasized each musical phrase in a different way; he touched the accordion the way he spoke of his friends—with mischievous and ever-renewed delicacy.

I was privileged to have a few accordion lessons with him and above all I liked his way of commenting on his own musical history: during the same session he successively played the dance of his early years, the one he had learned from his "fabulous friend" Pullone; then the one he had developed, which had earned him recognition some ten years back; finally his current dance, lively, complete, incorporating all the possibilities of the instrument.

His hand traveled over the entire keyboard and every silence was prolonged by an ornamental gesture: his slender fingers sketched the dance, even during its silent moments.

As I said earlier, Cambiadas had literally fallen in love with my accordion; he thought it had an "angelic" sonority and sighed with devout admiration when he played a few notes on it. On several occasions he had asked me to sell it to him and I regularly refused.

At the end of one of my visits one evening he asked a *regalo* of me; this was something—I understood that much from the start—that fell somewhere between a favor and a gift. He wanted me to lend him my accordion for the weekend, for two or three days, or maybe just for the day on Sunday when he was invited to the wedding of a very dear friend's daughter; he wanted the guests to hear the instrument, to share the pleasure of it with them, and finally, he wanted it for his own enjoyment.

I naturally agreed to his request. I was honored by it. We had only to iron out practical matters.

At that time I was staying in Orgosolo. I wanted to avoid having to return to his house for the *regalo* alone. I would have to travel only some twenty kilometers on the small, white dust—covered road, but it was better to avoid needless trips and to use the local bus; the driver was a friend of his. This option, however, was not possible: the bus didn't run on Sunday; consequently it was better that I drive back myself.

o

I returned for the day on Saturday and raised an issue that, as will soon be seen, became a considerable problem: I wanted to have a replacement accordion. I was studying accordion music, practiced it often, and a day did not go by when, during a chance encounter, I didn't ask other musicians to play it.

The problem became noticeably more complicated when, without his coming right out and saying so, I came to understand that Cambiadas was reluctant to lend me his own instrument. But one of his "very dear friends" would be able to lend me his. The friend in question was Peppino, who unfortunately three days earlier had lost his little seven-year-old nephew; he had accidentally been run over by a tourist. He was sure that under these tragic circumstances Peppino would not be playing any music, and probably not for a long time. It was equally clear that Peppino would agree to any request his friend Cambiadas might make. We had only to meet up with him. How should we proceed?

Cambiadas decided for me: I was to wait for him at his house. Besides, I could take advantage of the company of his father, quite stricken by old age, half-blind, and fairly deaf, and his mother, talkative and aggressive as many of the old women of Sardinia often are. He wouldn't be long; in fact, that very morning he was to go to the young boy's funeral with his "very dear friend." He would meet him there and would ask him to lend me his accordion.

He left right away; I waited for what seemed to be an eternity before deciding to go for a drive in the area, loading into my car, as usual, some boys who were hanging around and always ready to go for a ride, wherever it might be, just for the fun of it.

I went looking for cigarettes with the urgency of smokers or other obsessive types: a particular brand of cigarettes not to be found in Sardinia—unfiltered Gitanes. A rather odd urgency, considering that I had come only to collect an accordion and that the town was in mourning following the violent death of a child; and also considering that there was no chance of finding what I was looking for.

I returned to Cambiadas's house a good half hour later. Naturally he hadn't yet returned. His elderly parents hadn't moved an inch.

Gnawed by my usual desire always to be doing something, I looked for another way to keep myself occupied. I had a radio antenna that needed to be installed on my car. The car radio was not a luxury item among the various devices that contributed to turning my research in Sardinia into moments of pleasure. I received "Radio-Sopramonte," a local station bearing the name of the Orgosolo pasturelands, which, in addition to offering advice to those living in the mountains and a few recipes based on medicinal plants, played almost nothing but Sardinian music. The radio was an extension of and sometimes even aided my research. Listening to it I learned to recognize at the first notes the voices of the best singers and the playing of the best musicians. What is more, I had a connection to this radio station; it was run by some very young men to whom I regularly gave copies of my best recordings.

I went to a garage. All I needed was a screwdriver. The antenna installation quite naturally inspired those around me to improvise little scenarios. The boys who'd come with me proposed outrageous technical solutions, and as a joke called me "*ingegnere*"—engineer. When it came time to put the stem of the antenna into the hole in the body, there were plenty of comments in the international, heavily allusive language of boys.

Having mounted the antenna (to my great surprise, by the way, since it's rare that any odd job I undertake is successful), I returned to Cambiadas's house: I was eager to collect the "very dear friend"'s accordion. The friend was there. Cambiadas introduced us. They had both just come from the cemetery. We drank a glass or two of wine in an atmosphere now devoid of any reference to music. Other friends streamed in to join us after leaving the church. The comings and goings, the greetings and good-byes disturbed the normal flow of conversation.

We kept drinking. It was late by now and, since early morning, very few hours had gone by without a drink. Peppino, the "very dear friend," was magnificent. He had a calm self-assurance and intensely blue eyes. The abrupt loss of his little nephew seemed to have heightened his humanity. He clearly derived his aura from restrained and almost silent emotion. His slightest utterances immediately silenced the convivial background noise, even though nothing he said was of particular importance. His presence alone had the effect of a lapis lazuli in a landscape of rocks. Cambiadas took on a strictly ornamental function at his side. He went on and on about trivial subjects, and his naturally graceful speech turned into annoying chatter. My accordion, which was new at the time, held a place of honor on the table, like a sacred object. It was in the place where Cambiadas had left it that morning. As for myself, I wanted to see my transaction brought to a close, but it was hard for me to speak to Peppino. I was intimidated by his pain.

I prepared to leave, intending to put the question to Cambiadas as I was going out the door. I had had my query on the tip of my tongue for several hours. I really had to concentrate in order to sound natural and to have him believe my question was incidental.

I asked, "By the way, what about my accordion?" "It's right over there, as you can see," he instantly replied, indicating my own instrument sitting on the table. I cleared up the misunderstanding: "No, not that one, I know it's over there; I mean the one Peppino is supposed to lend me!"

A few kindly curses were addressed to the Madonna by way of a reply; he had forgotten my request.

We returned to the guests seated at the table. Cambiadas explained the problem to Peppino at length in an aside, as if he were discussing some shady dealing. He mentioned my love of music, his for my accordion, the need for a replacement, and argued for a long time before coming to the point.

Peppino seemed not to understand very well what he was talking about. The request was fairly complicated and unrelated to the day's events. To highlight what Cambiadas was asking, I intervened with a few smiles that I hoped appeared natural. Having waited so long, I was now more or less inclined to abandon the whole idea.

Peppino managed to hone in on my problem and finally understood what was being asked. No doubt to point out that he himself was involved in the exchange, Cambiadas offered to come with us to get the instrument. But now that Peppino seemed to have accepted the proposal, Cambiadas's presence was no longer necessary. Suddenly, under the pretext of needing to visit another friend, Cambiadas left us alone. It was already ten o'clock at night, and when we arrived at Peppino's house, my first instinct was to wait in the car for the accordion to be brought out to me. But naturally, that was not how things were done. I had to go in and sit down. Peppino brought out some wine and cheese, and although I was feeling the effects of fatigue and of too much drinking, we launched into a new conversa-

An *organetto* player. Abbasanta, 1980. Photo by Francesco Giannattasio.

tion. The little nephew came up at every turn. He was the best in the family. Indeed, at seven years old he had all the talent in the world, and notably a talent for music; he had already begun to play his uncle's accordion, the very one Peppino was going to lend me. Music connected the three of us, and Peppino would have very much liked to play for the little nephew, for himself, and for me, but he really couldn't; his close relationship with his brother prevented him from playing. This wasn't mere mourning, but rather a profound sympathy—almost a mental telepathy—which found its true expression only in silence.

I was invited to stay longer and to spend the night there, but I was reluctant to accept. I mainly wanted to be alone, a desire that always arose at the end of a long day of too much friendly companionship. I also declined for a very simple reason: the entire day had been devoted to an exchange of accordions, and I was determined to successfully complete the transaction and be on my way.

I pretended to have obligations in Orgosolo and, when it finally came time to leave, Peppino brought me the accordion, which was a common make, a Paolo Soprani of the worst sort—as heavy as lead—with which all the players in Sardinia at that time, including the best, made do. He told me he hadn't bought it for himself, but for his son. In fact, his son was beginning to play rather well (to "manage," was how he put it). We spoke for a moment about the musicians and the dances of Oliena—especially the old ones, which were very slow, whereas the dances of today were too fast.

I finally loaded the instrument into my car, very slowly going over all the vicissitudes of the day. I tasted the heavy night, encountered some shepherds ambling along and two or three herds of sheep without a shepherd. The air was cool and halfway back to Orgosolo I suddenly became curious to try out the accordion in the starry night.

While we were together Peppino had very succinctly warned me about the defects of the instrument. I had paid little attention, but I now discovered that it was in fact unplayable. The basses stuck together and with their thickly sustained notes masked the melodies of the right hand. I was disappointed, less by the instrument itself than by what its defects represented. They created discord and distorted the music, but more important, they also injured the delicate and confident relationship I thought I had established with the accordion's owner. I felt I had been swindled and above all did not understand how a man as subtle as Peppino could have agreed to such a shabby transaction. His lack of scruples troubled me.

At that moment I felt like going back to his house. Maybe I should go back to Cambiadas's instead, since he was at the origin of this blunder.

In other words, the defective accordion, the simple fact that one of its notes was stuck, had ruined the whole day.

My hesitations on the road, however, made a return to Oliena increasingly improbable. I went back to Orgosolo, to the "Petit Hôtel," where I was staying. Graziella, the owner, as was her wont, was keeping vigil (no matter what time I returned, the window of her room was always lighted).

I carried in my various bags, tape recorder, and microphones, and immediately settled down to repair the instrument. A spring was broken. I replaced it with a rubber band, which seemed to work. With this makeshift repair job my disappointment was in part eased. I went to bed and fell asleep.

o

The rubber band served its purpose for a long time. I saw the accordion again the following year in the same condition in which I had left it. Peppino's son had given up playing. As for the father, he no longer played either.

Cambiadas, overwhelmed by his friends and his meetings, and completely committed to his life of seduction, made even less time for me than usual that year. I didn't even have an opportunity to record his repertoire. In any case, he probably didn't want me to. He had gone into a new line of work, all the while continuing to play from fête to fête, but less frequently than in the past: he was selling used cars and took the risk of selling them to his "dear friends." He was less obsessed with acquiring my accordion than he had been the year before. On the other hand, he had opinions on my car, and gave them to me regularly. But beyond the realm of business, there was less of an urgent need for us to get together. As for myself, I very rarely worked on the repertoire of dances any more, and the few times we met, our conversations were superficial and had nothing to do with music.

I got out of the habit of visiting him, and gradually forgot to make my presence known, neglecting to send him the usual Christmas card and good wishes for the New Year.

ORGOSOLO

THIS WAS MY THIRD WEEK IN ORGO-
SOLO. THREE LONG, SEDENTARY AND HU-
MORLESS WEEKS STAYING AT GRAZIELLA'S
PETIT HÔTEL.

Graziella was living in a condition of semi-
widowhood: her husband Giuseppe was in
prison in Nuoro, the big town in Barbagia; he
would be there for another ten years. Implicated in a case of Sardinian-style
abduction, he had failed in the difficult task of laundering dirty money. I
had never met him, but I knew who he was as he had come to France with
singers from Orgosolo on several occasions. He himself didn't sing, but he
was a friend of the little choir of "shepherds" who for fifteen years had
brought the singing of Barbagia to continental Italy and even to France.

In fact, of the four singers who made up the choir only one had been a
shepherd for a brief time; that was Pasquale, who, incidentally, spoke very
little about that period in his life.

It is interesting to note that in Sardinia the profession of shepherd does
not necessarily imply long periods of isolation in the mountains or a required state of symbiosis with the animals. During the summer they don't
need much supervision; the animals give a rhythm to the lives of their
keepers but do not require their constant attention. One's duties as a shepherd are not all-consuming; moreover, the post is often temporary. It is
not uncommon to be a shepherd for a brief time in one's life.

In any event, the life of the shepherds constantly infuses the streets of
Orgosolo. Italian scholars, always eager to create concepts with magical-
sounding names, describe this situation in terms of *pastoralismo
ambientale*—"environmental pastoralism."

The amount of free time the shepherds have, evident in their frequent presence in the village, is often connected to stories of theft, both real and legendary, in Barbagia. There is in any case no doubt that it encourages such stories. In a certain sense herds are allotted in proportion to the amount of time one spends taking care of them. In Orgosolo, even though, of course, everyone knows which animals belong to whom, the need to assign the livestock to a specific owner is not always felt; this must be seen as resulting from the laws of a still active communal way of life.

Shepherds are continuously passing through the village, or stopping in bars to exchange a few words. They go to and from the pasturelands by car; the size and condition of the car give a rather precise idea of the size of the herd; hired hands generally drive only a motor scooter . . .

o

In contrast to the noisy life of the street, Graziella, owner of the Petit Hôtel, was strangely silent. She had visibly interiorized her husband's thefts and concealments and in turn seemed to have incarcerated herself.

The Petit Hôtel was an isolate, run in an atmosphere of mystery. But I was greatly pleased to sense I was one of Graziella's friends. Which made me wonder how her lucid morality, her distaste for concession, which was evident in her behavior, and especially her silent power over household matters did not immediately make our relationship an explosive one. I always felt I was on the verge of an outburst and found it difficult to ignore the brutality with which I saw her address her other clients. Perhaps that was the root of all the pleasure I derived from our relationship: the more disagreeable Graziella had been during the day with others, the more I felt privileged and liked by her.

Never once did she raise her voice to me. Our conversations, however brief and banal they might have been, were intense. But because of the pervasive tension, I was always afraid they would contain something to which I would be unequal. In any case, no matter what I did, a sense of impropriety interfered constantly in our relationship without my really knowing why.

Against this background of clandestine fear and unexplained complicity, I felt deep relief when, in the course of my research, I was led to work with Graziella's brother-in-law, Antonio, brother of her imprisoned hus-

band. He was an accordionist or, more precisely, *the* accordionist of Orgosolo, that is, the first musician people sought for all patron saint fêtes to
provide music for dancing, as well as the recognized artisan of a style
unique to the village.

Alone on the square for several hours he played the Orgosolo *ballu*, or
dance, which he had created himself from a relatively simple traditional
pattern.

That particular year Antonio almost never played. He was seriously ill
and was allowing his accordion, like himself, slowly to deteriorate. His
extreme fatigue had led him to simplify his playing (I knew this because I
had some of his early recordings). With advancing age he had lost the ability to perform his most dazzling musical flourishes, but he had retained
the essential variations of the dance, some of them learned from his father,
others created by him in his youth.

Our conversations, which for a time took him away from his great
suffering (he died the following year on 15 August, while the whole village was in celebration), were deeply sad. But at least on the first day I
was overjoyed at the idea of being able to tell Graziella something about
them. When I got back to the hotel I would be able to tell her things that
would fill the silence and neutralize the intimate violence of our relationship.

o

Thus on that night I made the first move. I anticipated success based on
the element of surprise. I had had access to Antonio, if I may say so, without her consent, and she most likely knew nothing of my visit to her
brother-in-law.

I knocked on her door, under who knows what pretext, to speak to
her. Always elegantly but simply dressed, she was busy with her household chores; but with the first sentence I uttered to broach the subject I
sensed that she would hear nothing of whatever I might say regarding her
brother-in-law. I was abruptly bringing to life characters who were too
close as well as, through her brother-in-law, the presence of her husband.
As I was trying to find my first utterances, my status as a foreigner became
all too evident. I was getting tangled up in my words just as Graziella's

eyes were clouding over. Any prospect of a conversation was lost. Nothing could be retrieved.

With Graziella's eyes definitively hidden away, I was at a loss, and returned, baffled, to my room. Our silences were immodest; the nonsilences became scandalous.

The next day I resorted, in a somewhat cowardly way, to playing at a rather high volume the recordings I had made of Antonio the day before. There was no response. I opened my door on several occasions and created activities that required me to go down the hallway. To no avail. Graziella was more absent than ever.

o

My days in Orgosolo were primarily spent at Pasquale's: lunch, a little nap at his house, discussions, rounds of drinks in bars, and then, unless I managed to steal away, dinner as well (in which case, we'd spend the evening at a bar).

That daily routine took its toll on me, but it was difficult to avoid it. I was the victim of a sequestration of sorts: the obligation to eat and drink could not be escaped.

One evening, tired of how regular and abundant our meals had been, I asked my hosts for some time off, for their permission to leave without dinner. Pasquale's wife, Clementina, made me take a plate of buttered pasta back to the hotel, something I could not refuse to do.

As for the rounds of drinks in the bars, I was truly tired of them. I was slowly becoming an alcoholic. Thanks to my lack of habit and the heat of August, I alternated between a stomach ache and illness. I did learn—unfortunately a bit late—that mineral water was on the list of acceptable drinks. By ordering water I was for a time sheltered, if not from requests for an explanation, at least from stomach cramps.

My only moments of freedom were the evening outings in the little customized truck, the *pulmino*, in which the choir of singers drove from festival to festival. Pasquale, who was the group's soloist, took the front seat. The rest of us piled in the rear. Pasquale, serious and concentrating on what he would be singing that evening, was as quiet as the driver, whereas the back of the truck turned into a canteen where we constantly im-

A tenore singing in a bar. Orgosolo (1983).
Photo by Bernard Lortat-Jacob.

provised amusing stories and ironic *strofette*—little poetic verses—
accompanied by dance rhythms.

The choir regained its dignity and gravity only upon arriving in the
village where it was to perform and when the singers put on their magnificent costumes in an atmosphere befitting the dressing of priests. I would
often be present at the meticulous dressing ritual carried out with slow
movements, both clumsy and precise. Thick, muscular bodies, sunbaked
from the neck up and the upper arms down, wide and white at chest, belly,
and back level, were enveloped in pleated linen and feminine embroidery.

The long hours spent with Pasquale in the kitchen whose shutters were
always closed (the large formal living room, as was the case everywhere in
Sardinia, was always off-limits) taught me a great deal. Although it was
Pasquale who, in a low voice, invited me every day, it was in fact to his wife
Clementina's house that I went. Clementina was the caricature of a Sardi-

nian woman. If I remember correctly, she was originally from Piedmont; perhaps her exaggerated behavior came from a desire to overcompensate.

In her wake a hurricane blew almost permanently over the house. She was either absent (and even then Pasquale seemed to fear raising his voice) or noisy.

She determined not only how the household was run but also the behavior and attitudes one was to assume upon crossing her threshold; she created fair weather and rain and, quite literally, heat and cold. We would be working with Pasquale when she would burst into the room declaring it was hot—we needed to take off some clothes—or cold—she brought along extra garments.

Once I thought I would foil her vigilance as mistress of the house with a perverseness that might be attributed to a reflex of defense.

We were having coffee served in very pretty matching cups. I had noticed, however, that the handle of the cup Clementina had given herself was slightly chipped. While she was fixing the coffee and was busy elsewhere, I reversed the order of the cups and put the chipped one in front of me. I had changed the order of things. It was only when the coffee had been served that Clementina became aware of the mistake (she did not suspect a plot). She made me give her my coffee and my cup. The cup disappeared forever from the everyday service. In the following days coffee was served in other cups, not as fancy, but again all matching.

Clementina's sentences were all in the imperative mood. But although feminine authority is wholly natural in Sardinia, in her case it seemed a little artificial, and really in part contrived.

I was able to verify this several times when Pasquale expressed a certain reticence about something. His wife then began to laugh. The protest, understood and turned into complicity, was a moment of grace. They had fun with accepted strategies and pretenses; I took pleasure in prolonging the laughter—perhaps in order better to understand it.

o

In an attempt to escape my obviously infantile situation as a forced guest of Pasquale and Clementina, I had come up with the idea of our doing something together.

Quite simply, I proposed putting my car and my time at their disposal for an errand or an outing of their choice.

The idea was accepted and we decided to go to Dorgali near the sea one day during the week. I was delighted with the plan, especially since I hadn't had a chance to swim in the sea for several weeks. But the idea of being able to do something for Pasquale and Clementina made me even happier.

The plan was to visit one of Clementina's cousins. She would spend the day with her, and Pasquale and I would go to the beach; for Clementina it was out of the question even to have a look at the sea.

We were to leave very early, before six in the morning, ostensibly to avoid being on the road in the heat (even though we were only going about forty kilometers), but mainly because everything out of the ordinary had to be undertaken early.

Our departure went smoothly. Clementina was quiet as soon as she stepped out of the house. Her silence went hand in hand with Pasquale's rediscovered self-assurance; every bend in the road—or almost every one—had a story behind it, and twice we had to visit friends' gardens on the way.

We dropped Clementina off at her cousin's house and after a brief visit Pasquale and I went off to the beach as planned. I took a quick swim while Pasquale, perched on one buttock, waited for me on top of some tall rocks, as if being near the sea disturbed him. I thought he was impatient to get back to see his wife and her cousins, but apparently such was not the case. He was master of a period of time that I knew nothing of, took me to a few bars in Cala Gonone and to the home of a friend. It consisted of a series of superimposed stones forming a hut, sheltering a sumptuous pink bathroom in which, due to the usual drought, there was no water.

o

Back with Clementina and her cousins, the situation had scarcely evolved. Several friendly guests insisted that Pasquale introduce himself. Recognized as a singer, he was obviously proud to be seen as such in my presence.

There were a lot of people present; it was a crowd rather than a reception. However, Clementina wasn't there. She had been whisked away by the women of the house and—putting her doubly beyond our reach—taken to see her relatives along with the other women. I understood only after an hour or two that there was no point in trying to get her back. Because I had a preconceived notion of what a visit should be, I was growing impatient. The interminable discussions in Sardinian, of which I understood nothing, and the very fact that, strictly speaking, they didn't seem settled in that house, and, finally, the impression of not being the guest of anyone in particular made waiting intolerable.

Enduring this state of affairs for another hour succeeded in doing me in. It was hot; I no longer knew why I was there. The *Vernaccia*, with which the middle class readily replaced the local wine, began to get to me. I wanted to escape. Which is what I did, under the pretext of wanting to visit one of the rare makers of Jew's harps: a very young man who had learned everything from his father before he died. I remember his delight when I showed him a whole book devoted to the instrument. With just a glance he memorized all the types of Jew's harps existing in the world, from Africa to Asia. He added his own insightful commentaries, then presented me with two harps with which he was not too displeased.

He played them for a long time before giving them to me, wrapping them up in yellowed newspaper and commenting at length on their respective qualities; he played the low-pitched one in the evening from the window of his workshop when he was alone. The sound, reverberating off the walls of the small, narrow street, became full and round. The high-pitched one was made for dance music. He had tried it out on the square: with electronic amplification the instrument's thin sound became powerful; it inspired dancers and, he said, "stole their feet away." With this Jew's harp the *ballu brincu* (the "jumping dance") became irresistible.

o

I was still basking in the young man's charm when I returned to the cousin's house.

The atmosphere there was exactly what it had been when I left. Nothing had changed. Pasquale, now seated on a low wall, seemed hardly to recognize me. After the exclusion of which I was at first the victim, there followed an obvious disapproval. It hit me all the harder as I had rejoiced in advance at the idea of telling Pasquale about the wonder of my discoveries. But apparently in his view I shouldn't have left—even if it was for a good cause—and I got nothing but slightly annoyed indifference from him.

In the meantime, nothing happened. Clementina had still not returned. It was late afternoon. I felt I was being mistreated and reacted with a second escape. This time into my car; I needed to take refuge. With the sun now low on the horizon, and with the radio that in this region played Sardinian music almost continually, my convertible was the best place to be. I felt both calm and in my rightful place.

After a while Pasquale inquired about my absence and came to find me. I had to go back in; my taking refuge was interpreted as an intention to leave.

I was anxiously assessing the extent of the damage done when Clementina reappeared. She probably thought I had spent the whole day in the car.

o

We left. Sadness overwhelmed us; my feelings of guilt were enormous. Clementina, seated next to me, said nothing.

After some ten kilometers during which not a word had been exchanged, a tear rolled down her cheek. It was the first silent action I had ever known her to perform. I had heard her laugh; I was now watching her cry. I had only one desire; to take her in my arms and ease her pain and my distress.

Something had to be done. I suggested a detour to the beautiful springs of Su Cologone. We could at least watch the cooling water flow and ease the stifling heat of the evening. That detour was even more painful than what had come before.

Contrary to what I had hoped, Clementina preferred to stay in the car, which enabled Pasquale to join me alone, talking incessantly about those magical springs, the most beautiful in all Sardinia and perhaps in all of Europe. (Mentioning Europe was obligatory whenever a value was placed

The procession of August 15. Orgosolo (1979).
Photo by Bernard Lortat-Jacob.

on Sardinia.) I counted the interminable minutes spent alone with
Pasquale. Clementina was waiting for us.

o

We drove off again in silence; the situation had not really changed. It
was almost dark. We had scarcely arrived when Clementina entered her
house with her usual vigor. She successively complained about how stuffy
it smelled (the windows had to be opened) and of the flies (they had to be
closed). In spite of our fatigue and the tensions of the day, there could be
no question of skipping dinner. Only the late hour authorized us to make
do with leftovers.

Pasquale rather quickly dragged me off to the square: For a stroll and a stop at the bar, of course. In this way I somewhat regretfully avoided Clementina's violent silences, and those, resigned and intense, of Graziella.

Before we left, Clementina caught up with us in the stairway to tell us not to catch cold. She gave her husband a sweater along with some money, which she unabashedly took from a little change purse to pay for our round of drinks.

○

In the comings and goings of the evening, the din of the motorcycles, the *motocarrozzelle,* and the dust-covered cars that had just arrived off the little mountain roads was overwhelming. As they were every evening at the same hour, Graziella's forever-closed windows at the Petit Hôtel were lighted. The street was the noisy world of men. The house was the world of women, where each one went to shelter her pain.

That night, the very closeness of such pain made it impossible for me to sleep. Until the soft noises of morning. Furtive and feminine noises. It was communal baking day when, as happened each month, Graziella, Clementina, and several women from the neighborhood assembled around the oven of a large house to make their men's bread.

Muravera

"You were right to come; you will learn something about Sardinia."

With these words, and a big smile, Attilio Cannargiu welcomed us.

It was during my first trip to Sardinia. Accompanied by a friend, I wanted to hear a player of the Sardinian clarinet, the launeddas. We were told to see Attilio. It was something of an odd idea to send us to him, for Attilio was relatively unknown; he lived right next to the best musicians of the country but was himself one of the poor and the obscure.

"I will tell you all about music, the music of the launeddas." These words eased a strong apprehension I had: This was my first interview with a Sardinian musician. I had just come from Morocco, having finished several years of research on musical practices that were commonly held secret, practices involving intrigues that had constantly to be unraveled.

In Morocco research necessarily proceeds by way of ruse and evasion. The point of view (and the very presence) of the interviewer is in any event displaced. Moreover, the music of Morocco (at least the mountain music I so loved) could not be commented on; it was played, that is all. When it was played badly, those in attendance had recourse to endless, often violent discussions. Anything could be brought up then, anything could be spoken of, with the exception of music. Then, when the arguments ceased, the playing continued, until the next hitch . . .

What I was to discover in Sardinia, among other things, was a delight in the spoken word and, as far as music, poetry, and dance were concerned, a natural inclination toward the explicit.

In less than thirty seconds a launeddas player had opened his door. That seemed an accomplishment in itself (the craziest stories are told about musicians and their exaggerated jealousies). He opened up his cellar and his wine and smilingly offered me knowledge that I had believed was inaccessible. It is an understatement to say he offered it; rather, he imposed it. We were there to understand.

What we were to understand was contained in the second part of his introductory sentence: It was simultaneously history, his history, his various launeddas, music, his music, and Sardinia. The amalgam was created from the start. It pervaded the interview from beginning to end as well as our subsequent conversations. For Attilio, the history of music was indistinguishable from the history of the launeddas, and the history of the launeddas from his own life.

o

The man was short, round, and stocky. His eyes had a sparkle and an energy that I had observed nowhere else. Having traveled on both sides of the Mediterranean, I presumed to believe that where brilliant eyes were concerned, the list had been drawn up and completed. Attilio demonstrated (as later, Pietro Nannu from Lodè, for example, would do) that nothing was further from the truth.

The eyes of a Sardinian look at you without contemplating you. They haven't the insistent sensuality of Moroccan eyes. Nor do they have a coquettish intent, only to steal away suddenly in fleeting shame. Sardinian eyes do not suggest possible relationships but rather affirm those that already exist and, beyond that, grant you an existence. I believe it is owing to the quality of those eyes and the way they look at you that I have never been bored here.

o

The room we were in was the one used to receive guests. We remained in it a short while, for the time it took to finish a bottle of wine.

Attilio's domain was in an adjoining building located at a slightly lower level. He took us to it. The first room we entered was very small. It was filled with stacks of yellowed newspapers, piled up or stuck on the walls. Attilio's history was in this room. It was here that he saved newspaper clippings pertaining to him. The Sardinian newspapers portrayed him as the last launeddas maker, heir to a great tradition. Or else they referred to the fêtes where he had played. There were few truly recent articles. He seemed to have retired from the active world a long time ago already. But his life's story assembled in its entirety in this room, was one that others had bestowed upon him: it was, in an often pompous and banal journalistic language, what had been written about him.

He had also preserved several letters from foreign scholars or curious tourists from the continent. As Attilio was practically illiterate, he had his son read them to him. He had underlined (or had had underlined) the titles and positions of his visitors and correspondents—almost all of them *professori*. He had also marked those passages where he was mentioned in a complimentary way.

We read these chronicles. The best ones were missing. Attilio looked for them. And yet it was he who had put them away. He found them: he was "the uncontested expert of the launeddas," the "ornament of Sardinian culture." His eyes lit up when he heard these things. They were speaking about him. We had been alerted. There was a photo of him; he was playing in front of some children and was wearing a splendid traditional costume, self-conscious in his borrowed finery: "I look like an idiot in that thing," he noted. The costume, which musicians still wear today when they perform in public, smacked of artifice. Attilio never wore it except on very special, rare occasions. Dressing up ill became him. It was only a representation, consistent with what could be seen in the first room of his house—the focus of all outsiders' eyes.

It was elsewhere that he worked, sheltered from those external presences, in an adjoining building where not even his wife was granted access.

o

We entered into an initial, cluttered space—his "museum." The walls were entirely covered with instruments—"all of which I've made," he pointed out.

When he took the time to do so, his son used a knife to engrave his father's name on the different instruments. His markings also provided technical information intended to distinguish them from each other. Two or three suitcases sitting on the ground were opened up for us. They contained instruments from times past. Two of them came from some former masters; the others he had made in his youth, when, as he put it, "he didn't know anything yet"; he added, "these instruments have no music," which, as I later understood, didn't mean they didn't produce any sound but that they were not made according to the system that Attilio had established over the years. For that reason they did not deserve to be displayed and were packed away into suitcases as they were in his memory.

○

The workshop was to the rear of the house. It seemed to turn its back on all the other rooms. It did not open onto the inner courtyard of the house, but onto an outdoor area piled up with recently cut canes. A door made of openwork fencing opened onto the natural setting of a hillside. It was here, every day, from dawn to evening and in every season, that he worked. He was seated on a low chair, much like the ones that were once found throughout Sardinia; his fine goldsmith's movements seemed inconsistent with the size of his body.

His only tools were two patched-up knives. A few sketchy diagrams were pinned to the wall. In a corner he had stocked his basic materials; they were elementary but all he needed to create instruments of great elegance, entirely made of hard canes: string for ligatures, wax to assemble the pipes and the reeds—indeed, simple reeds. That is all.

Three worlds coexisted in Attilio's house. The sitting room, where his wife lived and where he first brought us, was a neutral space. It was located near the kitchen. He never went into it except for meals. He received visitors there for a brief moment, the time it took to drink a glass of wine or two, before a conversation bearing exclusively on music could really begin. The other rooms were used for his work: the first was devoted to his archives; it contained letters from *professori,* newspaper articles, and all the official testimonies authenticating his knowledge. All visits began in this room. The second room—his museum of instruments—in turn testified to past work: that which could be shown was displayed on the walls; that which had to be hidden was put away in suitcases. The hidden work was that of his early years or the work of others, of *maestri,* to which Attilio granted little importance. The third room—the workshop proper—without being a completely secret place, had a more private character than did the others. I did not, moreover, have access to it until my second visit. Literally embracing nature, turning its back on social spaces and places for display, it confined Attilio in an industrious solitude.

For the moment we were in the "museum"; Attilio told us what he knew in a speech that was studded with technical terms that he delivered in short bursts. He had discovered music without anyone's help, and no one had ever taught him anything; that much was certain. He did not acknowledge any master; that much was unusual. For twenty years he had worked alone, far from the noisy squares where musicians normally assembled, far from those who, according to him, claimed to know everything and who all shared the common trait of being accused of pillage. In Sardinia intellectual property is abducted like sheep in the mountains.

I timidly mentioned a few names of known musicians, only to feed the conversation and show that I knew something about the subject. Each name unleashed a fury of appropriate curses. In fact, Attilio's colleagues were grouped into two categories: the dead and the living. The former had his good wishes since, compared with the latter, they had the advantage of not being able to elicit his jealousy.

Antonio Lara and Efisio Melis were among the former. They were respectable, but their respectability came only from their inoffensive qualities. Attilio mentioned them for the few compliments they had paid him before they died. The others—the living—were dangerous. The hatred they induced was proportional to their prestige. Attilio, as will have been readily understood, tolerated badly the glory of others—a stolen glory, in his opinion, which increased his own isolation, rendering it even more dramatic.

o

By refusing to have any musical affiliation, and by denying the nature of traditional knowledge, Attilio seemed to have created the conditions of his solitude himself. He labored entire days in his workshop, cut the canes and conducted his experiments all alone. Beside him there sat a little transistor radio held together with rubber bands and bristling with electrical wires. Through a haze of static interference, it played continuously, encumbering the air with modern sounds and Continental music. Attilio's relationship with the world was an essentially musical one.

He knew how to reproduce the music that came over the radio. Rather than the music itself, it was more the sound of the instruments that he imitated: the guitar, the trumpet, or the violin.

Nature, which he had learned to appreciate in the past when he was a peasant and whose constant echoes he heard from within his workshop, provided him with another source of inspiration. First the birds: the lark, the thrush, the owl, and others with Sardinian names whose equivalents I haven't been able to find in either Italian or French; the barnyard; insects—especially beetles and June bugs. Finally, the wind in the canes, the night air, and the rustling of the trees.

But it would be wrong to believe that this imitative research abandoned Sardinian music along the way: the lark and the thrush sang the notes of the launeddas, and Attilio's beetles all danced Sardinian dances. There was nothing natural about them.

Ultimately Attilio imitated only himself; his bestiary had no distinct boundaries. For him music was an intimate and essentially mental experience. It existed, moreover, only through inalienable gifts: "*Tutta la mia natura,*" he said—"It is all in my nature." As for its expression, it passed through a quasi-supernatural mediation, that of dreams.

Attilio dreamt of music. I asked him how that was possible. He assumed an astonished look, seeming to say: "Ah! You see, I am not like everyone else!" He dreamt of the music that surrounded him and heard it in his sleep. As soon as he got up (very early, as I had occasion to note in the following years when I slept over at his house), he played what the night had prepared for him.

o

Attilio was not just the interpreter of a world of sound to which he was made sensitive by his unique gifts; every day he practiced a sort of musical exorcism. A certain expression crossed his lips regularly: "*tirare fuori,*" literally, "to draw out." What he "drew out" was music, present in all things.

His goal was to construct every single launeddas, in all possible tonalities. Only the fulfillment of this ambition would put an end to his feverishness. In fact, what he wanted to do, despite its apparent conceptual simplicity, was of immense complexity for him. For several, somewhat technical reasons.

The Sardinian launeddas is tuned in a number of scales fixed by partly convergent traditions. In the course of his research (and unfortunately for him) Attilio discovered the new possibilities offered by the temperament and the division of the octave into semitones. But the musical temperament bequeathed to us by the eighteenth century and that of Attilio were not very much in tune.

For a time he had undertaken a practice that was formally correct but musically absurd: knowing that the seven notes of the scale could be altered in two ways (sharps and flats), he attempted to assign not twelve tones to an octave but twenty-four. In this undertaking "the flats are hard to find," he confessed, and "difficult to bring out." At present, he was inclined to believe that the scale included fourteen tones (he counted several times in my presence and, time after time, arrived at different numbers). The theoretical result was contrary to what his ear told him. One day I will help him put some order into his theoretical adventures. For the time being I am learning.

o

For Attilio, "*la musica è quattro*" — "music is four." He couldn't stop counting. Such is the price of knowledge.

He used four families of instruments, each having its own mode of tuning. In fact, using his fingers he counted five or six. In any event, based on this uncertain foundation there were numerous combinations since each instrument was made out of three pipes.

Four families, three pipes each, a number of tones estimated at thirteen, fourteen, or twenty-four, each figure multiplying with the other: the number of instruments he needed to construct reached several hundred, at least if my calculations were more exact than his.

○

When he wanted to make an instrument in a given key (that year he was on A-flat and would proceed to A-sharp the following year), Attilio started with a base, a fundamental tone, by blowing into the longest pipe, the *contrabassu,* as he called it. This pipe gave only one low note. He blew into it for several hours before starting to construct the other two, which were to be in harmony with it.

From then on I understood why in his mouth the sound, the instrument, and the cane that enabled its creation were synonymous. The sound was born of the instrument; the music was born of the sound and was devised from it; but the process was one and the same.

Attilio's feverishness was fed by the intensity of his listening, and that listening by the intensity of his blowing. The blowing itself, long and uninterrupted, generated an indescribable ecstasy.

The music was "already there," he asserted, as if he wanted to isolate a few sounds from a single spectrum. I heard only a single note, beautiful and profound. He insisted. All the while playing, he tried to convince me with his eyes. To increase the resonance he put a drinking glass at the end of the longest pipe. This was his *microfono* (he pronounces it *miclofono*). For this he had a dozen or so glasses, of all sizes, which were the only truly domestic objects in his workshop. Turning them one way or another, he obtained different harmonics. Depending on the positions, and also on the shape of the glasses, the spectrum was decomposed and recomposed like an anamorphosis. He forced into his head what he would "draw out of it" later when he made the other pipes, the ones to be tuned to the first.

Along with Attilio I discovered the mental reality of music at the same time as its subjection to the rules of resonance. In the wide sound spectrum of the cane he blew into he sought what could be used for his musical ends. He calibrated and tuned his instruments from a single tone whose depths he endlessly probed. Nature had put into music things that one had only to "draw out." Sonorous matter formed Attilio's knowledge and his very concepts. By his side I felt as if I was witnessing what had been experienced by the first human beings as well as the very birth of the world. He discovered through empiricism, as if for millenia nothing had been tried before.

And yet I wondered how the components of a single sound could lead to a daily rapture of such intensity. Surely such rapture did not necessarily come out of renewal. It was equally born of the repetition of things, provided that such repetition was precise, rigorous, and conducted with fervor.

o

I have experienced similar attitudes in the company of fishermen friends from the Mediterranean who pulled the same type of fish out of the water every morning at daybreak. Their work, in spite of its necessary automatism, remained miraculous. Every fish pulled from the water inspired admiring comments that will undoubtedly cease only with the disappearance of the seas. These experiences, involving the same gestures and attitudes, weave together both ritual and everyday lives. It is no doubt the precision of the act's repetition that gives fishermen of the same species of fish and seekers of the same sound a feeling of eternity: every day in his workshop Attilio uncovered and discovered the same world. His entire endeavor consisted of ridding it of all darkness. When he achieved this, he was infused with what he called the "true feeling." The "true feeling," he said, was "when the head stops in order to make precise things," that is, things consistent with what nature reveals. At that moment, he confessed, he had been known to cry.

o

I have said a lot about the way Attilio thought and worked. Up until now I've had no need to mention the way he played. I must, however, say this: he was very awkward. It was most difficult for him to lead a dance to its conclusion, or even to develop a musical phrase. Attilio played the way he spoke—in sudden bursts—and the way he was—out of all measure. He sketched a melody, then without transition went into another. He was more infatuated by sound than by music. Seeing how hard it was for him to play, I was better able to measure the genius of others, of those he con-

47

sidered not as his rivals nor even as his colleagues, so jealous was he of them.

His true virtuosity was not in the realm of syntactics. It lay entirely in his ability to combine sounds in the moment. Only the superposition of acoustical spectrums was of interest to him. It was the object of his research. In the strict sense of the term, he was an expert in the matter.

On this occasion I came to realize that his musical gift was multi-faceted. Long exposure to the resonant pipes had given Attilio perfect pitch: he needed no standard to perceive pitches or to hear harmonic components. No doubt the plenitude of sounds had distanced him from conventional musical creations. In any case he didn't see the need for them.

o

A few years ago Attilio came to France to participate in a celebration of Italian folk culture. I had taken the risk of recommending him, knowing that, with the way he played, he would do little justice to Sardinian music; but he had become a friend.

During his visit he never slept. When he was staying with me, he strolled around in the backyard most of the night and got up well before dawn. He wanted to get to know France, that is, French flowers, insects, and birds. He communicated nothing of his observations to me. In the morning we were heading for Paris on the expressway (at that time I was living in the suburbs), and he asked whether that road went to Naples. I told him yes, but in the other direction. He then suggested that I turn around so we could go see his sister who had married a Neapolitan.

That same year we organized a trip for him to the south of France. He ended up in Clermont-Ferrand where he had decided to stop. He got lost in the city and didn't get back on the train.

He called to tell us that he didn't know what to do, but that all was well, that the air of Clermont was invigorating, and that it was better there than in France. The Sardinian companions who had gone with him had assured him that Clermont-Ferrand was in America. Pranks of that kind were all it took to feed his misanthropy. Even in France Attilio re-created the conditions of his isolation.

When I saw him at his house the following year, he didn't say much about his mishap, but he asked me to bring him a gift another time, something he had noticed during his trip but whose name he didn't know. From his description he wanted a drum.

Sometime later I gave him one that had come from Morocco. He asked only where the skin had come from (it was made of goatskin), and hardly looked at the instrument. He hung it on the wall in the room where he assembled his tributes and the testimonies to his glory. That gift made me part of his story.

Jerzu

Musicians and nougat vendors are experts in geography. They never need to look at road maps: they have memorized the different roads that take them from village fête to village fête and know all the shortcuts. As for musicians, who rarely own a car, they know the schedules and anticipated delays of public buses by heart.

Aurelio Scalas was to take the six o'clock bus to get to the procession in Jerzu where he was to play later that morning.

I knew three Aurelios: the one making the trip, silent, immobile in the early morning air, whose only baggage was a long cylindrical case containing his clarinets made of hard reeds; the domestic Aurelio who every morning played his *suonate* just for the pleasure of it, and who was busy the rest of the time in his garden. On this particular day, I met the Aurelio of fêtes.

His character underwent a true transformation upon reaching the final bends of the road announcing the entrance to the village.

Upon arriving, Aurelio, who was essentially a modest man, was forced to assume the air of a *signore*. In fact, his behavior was subject to two contradictory demands. As a fête musician he had to be cordial and warm, that is, he had to lose some of his apparent frostiness. But his first concern as he got out of the bus was to inspire respectability in order to show that he was worthy of the remuneration he was asking. As a professional Aurelio always connected his fees, the seriousness of his work, and the quality of his music. He expected appropriate compensation from his hosts— he did not want to sell himself short—and also assumed that he would be invited to the best home in the village. He rated the quality of the fête by the compliments he was paid. On the other hand, he could rant on forever

50

about the places, dates, and circumstances in which he was not shown the proper respect. Every invited musician expected to be flattered. About Aurelio it was said that he was a good launeddas player, but *to* Aurelio it was said that he was the greatest in all Sardinia.

o

"The greatest in all Sardinia"—this compliment was also being paid to one of his colleagues—Luigi Puntorgano—probably at the very same moment in another village. One never spoke of Luigi to Aurelio, nor of Aurelio to Luigi; but any allusion to the launeddas evoked this confrontation. If the two men shed light on each other in a conversation as do the two voices of a musical antiphony, in everyday life each man, without ever admitting it, suffered from the shadow cast upon him by the other.

Aurelio and Luigi's paths crossed in the southern hills of Sardinia. In Sarrabus together they shared a small market formed by a constellation of village squares to which both of them were invited to play.

As for Luigi Puntorgano, he embodied the two specialities of Sardinia: music and emigration. In fact, it was during the solitude of a long stay in Germany that he had worked on his brilliant, pure playing, of a moving and sometimes even excessive lyricism.

o

The procession in which Aurelio was to play fell in the category of manual labor. It required more physical endurance than true musical talent. Every year, exchanging the weak light of the small church candles for an hour in the summer sun, the Virgin Mary and various patron saints, carried by four men, went for a stroll in the town. The music, no doubt because it was essentially both sacred and secular, assured the transition from the church to the village and from the village to the church. Aurelio, who played without interruption, led the way for the divine images, the priest, and the women. The men brought up the rear of the procession.

That day it was the angel Gabriel that Aurelio, in shirtsleeves, went to get at the church. The gilded angel, somewhat weathered by time, was carried by men of unequal height so that it leaned to one side, one of its wings hitting the corners of buildings in the narrow streets.

Zio (uncle) Aurelio playing the launeddas in a procession after mass. Jerzu (1983). Photo by Bernard Lortat-Jacob.

In every religious fête Aurelio had an attentive ally: the village idiot. Like a character in the crèche, he was always present. Entranced with the movement created by the arrival of the music, he would move his arms frenetically; when Aurelio blew into his instrument, he would utter little cries.

The village idiot, who was never designated as such, was always an admiring and noisy commentator. An extension of the fête beneath a painful mask, he represented its excesses, and only became mute and silent again with a return to calm. He would always accompany me as I moved around a fête. Like me, he was attracted by what moved. We found ourselves once again side by side in the procession, near Aurelio.

We passed underneath balconies decorated with delicate flowers and in front of huge frescoes painted on walls against which the angel and his attendants stood out.

As he entered the church, Aurelio continued to play the same sweet music, destined for the angels, until the end of the mass, which was announced by the heavy and vulgar intervention of an out-of-tune harmonium.

On leaving the church a few dance steps might have been tried out on the square as they used to be in the past. This was almost never done anymore. Dancing was for the evening. But the habit of staying together for a long while after leaving mass remained. People stayed outside longer than they did inside, especially the men who, in little groups, started conversations that they would continue at the bar. The women stood impassively, their backs to the front of the church. They were silent and seemed to be waiting for the movement of retreat to begin on its own.

Bound that day to church matters, Aurelio remained among the women. While waiting for someone to invite him home he was now engaged in his first civilities. In the house to which he was invited, where we were taken, a half-dozen young men, stripped to their waists, turned sheep on spits. Owing to the quality of the reception, Aurelio took on unabashedly mundane airs. He flattered the women of the house and highlighted the value of his presence by calling attention to my own: I was a *professore* from Paris, I knew Sardinia better than he, I played the accordion like a Sardinian, and so forth. His exaggerations had a strictly diplomatic function; I am used to them by now.

Aurelio only spoke to the older women, not to the young girls whom he saw as children, whose charms he admired and whose presence he noted like an old art lover pointing out the delicacy of a well-known painting. The cooks, all shepherds, were dripping with sweat, and regularly came over to see how we were doing.

○

The meal had an agenda. It took place in the home of the prior of the festival, a rich man. The year before another *suonatore*—Luigi Puntorgano, in fact—had been invited. The idea was not to openly denigrate Luigi, but all the same Aurelio's position for next year had to be insured. Under these circumstances I better understood why I was there and why Aurelio was so happy to bring me with him; I attested to his supremacy and was to intervene at least indirectly in his favor to help him carry off invitations. While Aurelio was a feather in his host's cap, I was Aurelio's feather; this strategy made us accomplices.

The afternoon continued with a few visits in the village and ended with a coordinated movement toward the hub of the fête where the men of the festival committee were busy with final preparations.

The squares of Sardinia, located in the center of villages, are of modest proportions. And they appear to shrink even more each year as cars, new buildings, and the population of the country increase in number. Like the squares where he was invited to perform, Aurelio, when he played, seemed to shrink with the passing of time. The lack of attention of those listening to him had progressively altered his self-confidence, to the point that he was hindered in his ability to move his audience. His musical imagination must have suffered from it. To all appearances, playing demanded more of an effort from him each year.

That evening Aurelio appeared even more diminished than usual as he climbed onto the stage, for it was filled with huge speakers that announced the arrival of a group of young "pop" singers from the continent who would play later in the evening. The leader of the group, with dyed hair, had offered him the use of his sound system. The sound was deep, full, and overwhelming.

Aurelio had spent many long years learning how to adjust his reeds and, what is more, at the price of additional puffing, to choose the hardest ones in order to increase his volume. Now suddenly, he had more decibels than he knew what to do with, which made him play much louder than he was used to playing. He was no longer the only artisan of his music as the volume of the sound transported him and his launeddas into a world apart located far beyond the friendly conversations and the noises of the square. His isolation became even greater when the young Italian pop music lovers amused themselves by focusing green, red, and white spotlights on him. Aurelio couldn't hear his music, and now he could no longer see the dancers. His fingers, playing out of habit, flew over the instrument, but nothing could be sensed below. The music lost all its meaning and, under these conditions, Aurelio performed only the hackneyed parts of the dance.

When he was done performing, he raised his arms the way he must have seen it done on television and commented on his experience with humor. Then a young saxophone player came over and asked if he might play with him. Perhaps he wanted to prove that he could master the difficult form of the dances of Campidano. His playing was loud. In fact, although he had grasped the metric structure of the dance, he provided a poor caricature of it.

Aurelio spoke and gave details—it was now time for culinary metaphors: "A dance is formed like a menu; it has its first course, its spicy elements, and its different dishes. The whole must be gradually put together. If one gives too much music at the beginning, one chokes the client; on the other hand, a single dish does not make a meal."

A village woman was paying attention to these explanations, which, from what she could pick up, fell into her domain. She joined the conversation with a discreet laugh and left it once the metaphor had been exhausted and the culinary subject abandoned.

o

Aurelio's musical universe was made up primarily of interminable diatribes with his colleagues; but it also contained a body of principles that, in his opinion, the others were unaware of; their errors were proof of this. He owed the richness and the precision of his musical vocabulary to musicians who often came from continental Italy to visit and learn from him. His didactics were those of a *professore,* whereas his imagery was borrowed from everyday life, from poetry, and from the long trips he regularly made to the villages in the south of Sardinia. Using his finger, he outlined on the planks of the stage the diagram that the music had to follow to accompany the dance; he indicated a village, a road, a thicket, and commented: "Music is a geography; it has its passages, marked like those of a road one cannot leave; once the terrain has been crossed, it is impossible to go back the other way. It is foremost a route. Certainly, if the dancers are tired it is possible to take shortcuts and avoid the *fioriture;* but on the other hand, when the square is hot and they ask for more, one must think of all possible detours."

The Italian saxophonist had trouble grasping the comparison. Wanting above all to display his knowledge and to stress the importance of written music (and thereby his own importance, he who in a short while would go on stage), he threw a few technical terms out at Aurelio that, because they were incomprehensible to him, appeared insulting. I felt authorized to intervene. From my bag I took out a musical transcription of one of Aurelio's dance tunes and, to calm our companion, in turn threw a few pedantries his way.

Only through what is written down can one understand what a musical grammar truly is. I had undertaken to analyze the complex syntax of Aurelio's music and to determine, using the obligatory passages, what the possible musical escapades might have been. The research was not easy to conduct because Aurelio had a surprising ability to wander off the paths he himself had traced. From one moment to the next he never played exactly the same way. One found the same signposts on his musical landscape, but the music was constantly changing, like the flow of a thought in continual movement.

o

Demanding of himself, Aurelio was even more so of his colleagues. He never forgave a young man whom he had recommended to play at a fête several years ago for having played the wrong rhythm one evening (and only one time); this betrayed his confidence and, what was more, brought shame to all Sardinia. What could one expect of musicians who made mistakes? According to him, people would quickly exchange them for records or cassettes, and that would be the end of the profession.

To insure continuity—that was among his preoccupations—he had two students. Bearing the precious testimony of a knowledge acquired over many years, he gave a name to the tradition from which he had been nourished. The name of Aurelio Scalas was still known by two or three generations.

One of his students was breaking his heart: young and very gifted, he had unfortunately fallen in love.

Women caused great damage to Sardinian music: they distracted young men from rigorous training and invited old men to stay at home. Sandro (that was the name of the young man) ran around all day long like a fool on his motor scooter, hunting down his beloved wherever she was. He was forgetting about music.

The lessons took place without a word. Aurelio played, then passed the instrument to his pupil who had to repeat to the nearest *fioriture* what he had just heard. If Sandro did not succeed, Aurelio repeated the passage, rarely pointing out what the problem had been. One left the music as one had entered it, without transition or prelude. One knew where one was. The piece to be played was precise, entirely conceived before its performance. Music seemed to have the materiality of a statue that was temporarily missing an arm or a foot, and it was that arm or foot that was to be shaped during the lesson.

o

Talking about other launeddas players and himself Aurelio often used the concept *noi*, the "we." Excluded from this little circle were all those who were not *suonatori*, but only *soffiatori*, those who only "blew" into the instrument. The *noi* was bounded by rivalries, either latent or explosive, depending on the case. But there was a distinction solicited by all, which consisted of having a surplus of places where one was invited to play in order to distribute them generously to one's rivals. It was for this reason that Aurelio went to so much trouble to "have" the fête of San Gabriele of Jerzu: he had taken it away from Luigi the year before. His plan for the following year was to get himself invited to it once again in order, in the best of circumstances, to invent some excuse not to attend. He would then take great pleasure in offering the invitation to Luigi who would have to accept it secondhand. In this way he would score points against his rival.

Aurelio painstakingly filled in the calendar hanging on the wall of his kitchen. He conscientiously marked off the fêtes and noted in pencil those he intended to leave to others.

Luigi Puntorgano, for his part, did the same. Neither of them revealed his plans in advance. But a few years ago I was curiously surprised when I invited Aurelio to play in Paris, and he told me that I also had to invite Luigi. But Luigi refused, under the pretext that he had to go to Germany, or perhaps even to America.

THIESI

A SOCCER MATCH HAD GATHERED TO-
GETHER TWENTY-TWO PLAYERS AND ONE
REFEREE. BY HIMSELF THE REFEREE,
PIETRO, TOOK UP MORE SPACE THAN ALL THE
OTHER ATHLETES. HE TOOK UP THE WHOLE
PLAYING FIELD AND ENCOURAGED THE TEAM
FROM HIS VILLAGE. HE SMILED AT THOSE ON
THE OTHER SIDE TO SHOW THAT HE NOTICED THEIR PRESENCE—BUT DID
NO MORE THAN THAT. THE GAME SEEMED TO UNFOLD UNDER HIS DIREC-
TION. HE BORE RESPONSIBILITY FOR THE MATCH. THEY WERE PLAYING
NOT SOCCER BUT RATHER A GAME WHOSE RULES HE, THE REFEREE, AP-
PEARED TO BE CREATING, ALL OF WHICH GAVE HIM THE RIGHT TO IMPOSE
EXTRAVAGANT "CORNER KICKS," "PENALTY KICKS," AND "OFFSIDES." IN
BETWEEN TWO STRIDES THE BREAK IN ACTION GAVE HIM THE OPPOR-
TUNITY TO GO HUG A LITTLE NEPHEW HE HADN'T SEEN FOR A LONG TIME,
TO EXCHANGE GREETINGS, AND TO CARRY ON SEVERAL CONVERSATIONS
AT THE SAME TIME—CONVERSATIONS BEGUN WHILE THE GAME WAS UN-
DER WAY WITH WHOEVER WAS WHERE THE BALL WAS KICKED AT THE TIME.
FRIENDS WHO ALL WORKED AT THE LITTLE CHEESE FACTORY OF THIESI
WERE ASSEMBLED IN THE MIDDLE OF THE *CAMPO SPORTIVO.* NEAR THE
EIGHTEEN-METER LINE WERE THE INSEPARABLE COMPANIONS WITH
WHOM HE WENT FROM FÊTE TO FÊTE ON SUMMER EVENINGS. AND THE
YOUTH OF THIESI WERE ALL AROUND THEM. EVERYONE, OF COURSE,
KNEW PIETRO. AND PIETRO KNEW ALL OF THEM EVEN BETTER.

o

Pietro was a mailman. At thirty years old, like many young people of Sardinia, he still lived with his parents. His father, a barber and mandolin player, was in charge of the public telephone office, the *centralino*.

All communications in the village were transmitted through Pietro and his father, but in opposite directions: people congregated around the father's phone booth for outgoing messages—the expression *"centralino"* is indeed well chosen—whereas the son distributed the incoming mail from the little post office. Thus people went to the father (to make a phone call and perhaps to have their beards trimmed); the son came to their houses.

o

The fact that the village women did not go to the barber, although they did use the phone as much as the men, led Pietro's mother to open a hair salon behind the *centralino,* that is, in the family's house. If I remember correctly, the hairdryer, an impressively large "helmet"-style apparatus, was set right above the parents' double bed.

o

One day I was lucky enough to be able to deliver the mail with Pietro: a convenient way of coming into contact with all of Thiesi, its life, and its problems. I think I visited all the families in Thiesi, tasted all of their wines, and benefited from all their advice for successful social relationships.

Upon arriving at a house Pietro systematically stated the contents of what he was bringing as well as its origin. In this way he prepared each recipient for the news he was about to receive. He knew the contents of the envelope before it was opened, and announced, "It's your son who writes from Turin; he will tell you that he has not yet found a place to live, but that he's staying at Mario's" (he and Mario both worked at the Fiat factory). To someone else he brought a money order along with a Santa Claus smile.

Once a month the many pensioners in Thiesi awaited Pietro as if he were an envoy from heaven, and nothing could convince them of the contrary: his eternal smile, his strong, sonorous, melodious, and reassuring voice, his way of taking other people's concerns to heart indeed gave him a divine charm. He read letters out loud to old people who didn't have their glasses. As for the old women, they could never seem to find their glasses when Pietro arrived; this was not by chance: they loved his voice and wanted him to stay as long as possible. The letter was truer when Pietro read it. When it was written in Italian he translated the obscure terms; in every case he added useful commentaries, thus immediately preparing upon the first reading the appropriate response to be given.

Written in an old-fashioned, painstaking script full of ornate lettering, the outgoing mail was given to Pietro. He would suggest an addition, critique some phrasing, or point out an omission. If letters from Thiesi were very much alike and if they all mentioned the same things, it is mainly because the old people's problems were all the same, but it is also because they all bore Pietro's mark.

o

Soccer coach and referee, man of letters and postman, school *maestrino*—Pietro accumulated all these titles; but his great specialty was village fêtes. Pietro didn't miss a one.

He approached a fête as a conqueror, with an exemplary methodical mind. His goal was to see to it that everyone had a good time. Often his presence alone was enough to achieve this. He arrived early and conscientiously drank all evening long. He made himself available equally to everyone, and never forgot anyone.

He was always among the first to arrive, and never left before daybreak. I really began to worry when I was to ride back in his car with him after such an evening. He couldn't stand up, but he knew his limits. When returning from a fête his speed never exceeded ten kilometers per hour. In these frequent and regular situations he had imposed the rule on himself never to drive above first gear.

One night it took us more than two hours to cover the twenty-five kilometers that separated us from Thiesi. Several times a week we arrived at his house in time for the first cup of morning coffee.

It seems to me that I didn't sleep at all during those ten days I spent in

Thiesi, or only briefly under the olive trees using my tape recorder as a pillow.

During fêtes, whether in Moroccan communities or in Sardinia, sleep in any event never constitutes a right. It is seen, rather, as an infringement of an implicit rule that requires one to be open to everything except one's own discomfort. Similarly, to refuse a round of drinks or to excuse oneself from taking a spin in a car is considered almost illegal, as are the migraines that come from a repeated lack of sleep.

Pietro, who, moreover, worked during the day, informed me of the night's festivities around six in the evening; we had to awaken some young newlyweds, sing a serenade at a house, go hear "guitar song" (in fact, this was the goal of my trip), and visit with the fire watchmen, the men who from high up in the mountains day and night signaled the daily outbreak of fire. Depending on where we went there might be a few added "extras": we might participate in actually extinguishing a fire, or, more rarely, in watering a garden. Our plans were foiled by numerous urgent interventions. As for music, it necessarily came after everything else. Gatherings with musicians were constantly postponed, but the generous behavior that I learned from Pietro was irresistible. Exactitude was no longer the courtesy of kings; it was only that of cretins and egoists. As the days went by and extravagant plans were made and then abandoned, the number of blunders I accumulated on account of being constantly late no longer made me feel guilty. All the excuses I made were not only true but also good ones.

During those ten days I was doing no more than conform to an archetypal model, one that was exemplary in its very excesses. It was a question of responding without any restriction to the demands of the summer season of fêtes.

In the course of things I learned what a starry sky and a forest fire were. To look at the sky was above all to talk about the sky; the stars inspired infinite commentaries and, in some instances, poetry, sung by the shepherds and the fire watchmen. In fact, the latter were often themselves shepherds; they could be suspected of signaling the very fires that they themselves had lit, to clear the fields and better feed their animals, when they were off duty.

The stars and heavenly bodies brought to mind the absolute, love, and women; but women were never included in our outings. One day Pietro confessed to me that he and his companions were "*antisessuali*" ("anti-sexual").

In a certain sense love was incompatible with collective life. Lovers shut themselves up in their own affairs and no woman could tolerate, compounded with the discomfort of our nights, such excessive masculine outgoingness.

During the last few years, however, there were a few attempts that went against these principles, and two or three young women accompanied the men in their capacity as fiancées. That didn't last long; such arrangements could only have been temporary, leading either to marriage or a breakup.

o

In this atmosphere that excluded the fairer sex I was curious to see what a serenade would be like; therefore I was delighted to learn that we were going to "do" one that very evening in the village.

Everyone has a preconceived and romantic notion of a serenade: while the amorous allusion is borne by the erotic atmosphere of the night, the beautiful lady is on the balcony or in her room hidden behind the shades of her window; the aubade comes to disturb her tranquility. The indiscretion of the song and the fact that it is heard by her neighbors makes the intimacy even more scandalous. I was dreaming of it already. In addition I was the musician they needed. I would play the accordion and Pietro would sing.

I had been working separately on the three or four melodic formulas typical of the region, which enabled me to provide a basic accompaniment; owing to the frequent nocturnal follies of that period, I was so often asked to play that I was acquiring a natural mastery of the instrument and increasingly agile fingers.

We would do the serenade after the fête, around three in the morning, which seemed pretty late to me. I rather thought that the most propitious hour would be prior to midnight, before sleep set in, before the first dreams, the hour of fantasies. The fair lady ready for bed, in her negligee, the man and his exhilarated friends below . . . But I had definitively given up asking questions. In any event, before all of this took place we were supposed to go to Banari to attend the great "guitar song" competitions.

o

When we arrived in Banari the competition had already begun, in the center of a little square on a stage set up for the occasion. Each singer had his microphone, his voice, and his style. They were professional singers whose styles were obviously unrelated to that of the village.

I was very familiar with this music from having listened to a lot of it in Paris on old, scratchy records. But I had never seen it performed, in a certain sense transposed onto the stage. Immediately, the singing recovers its original physical and emotional sources. How can one accept that this music, or any other, be heard without being seen?

To the ear the timbre seemed to be made fragile by its power. The voice, strongly nasal and forced in the high notes, seemed ready to break. The eye, on the contrary, observed a perfect ease and mastery. The singing was both harsh and sweet. The singers looked more like city dwellers than peasants, and more Italian than Sardinian; their manner was exaggeratedly civil. From their bearing—but not their voices—they could pass for oratorio tenors. Their gestures were economical. No hands on their hips (that would appear common), nor at the ear (only peasants do that). Their arms hung down at their sides. The form of the music, which was the same for all the performers, adapted to various styles and the rule of the game required that each singer surpass his colleagues. The joust consisted both of taking over smoothly from the other and of surprising him with unheard-of ornamentation. Each variation had its own richness, which was commented on by the audience through murmurs of admiration and applause.

For anyone not yet familiar with this music, those noisy commentaries provided the key to an aesthetic. The admiring "oohs" and "ahs" were indications that had a pedagogical value: that evening I learned how to uncover beauty with certainty (that is, with the others) and strove to applaud at the right moments, until it became spontaneous and right.

I was hard at work making recordings, a task made difficult by the strength of the voices, attempting to limit the static introduced by a strident sound system. Pietro, flanked each time by a new group of friends, came over regularly to encourage me and to serve as referee in my difficulties, as he did on the playing field.

When there was a pause in the music he stepped up to the microphone to introduce me to the audience. With natural ease he explained what I had come to do in Sardinia. He told in great detail what I had explained to him in the course of our informal conversations. He mentioned my knowledge of the Moroccan mountainside, the life of Berber shepherds, and the price of their sheep. He went on like that for what seemed to me an interminable few minutes. I felt needlessly revealed. I sensed above all that to give so much importance to the story of an individual went against the grain of what I had experienced since I had arrived in Sardinia.

The Moroccan sheep did, however, have some success. Everywhere for the rest of the evening one heard snippets of conversations of which the Berbers in the Morrocan mountains were the central and primary topic. Strolling around with Pietro from group to group I was asked to clarify such and such a technical point concerning the life of the people and their animals. The usual amount of free time the men enjoyed, their natural attraction to travel, the eagerness with which my accounts were received, and finally the help of the *Vernaccia* led to grand plans to be carried out the next day. But that next day never came. I suppose that the very idea of conquest or the Crusades was born from such oneiric jousts as these.

o

It was late. I reminded Pietro incidentally of our serenading commitment. It took me another full hour to tear him from what seemed to be his natural milieu and at the customary speed we returned to Thiesi, stopping directly in front of a house opposite the church.

I asked Pietro for details about the lady we were to awaken. It turned out it was not a lady. It was Antonio-Maria, an old pal who, at almost forty years old, should have thought about getting married. Or more precisely, Pietro and his friends had thought it would be a good idea for Antonio-Maria to think about it.

Thus the goal of the serenade was not to establish a pact between lovers, but publicly to compromise someone who could be so compromised. As for the intended, she was totally absent and perhaps even nonexistent. This was the publication of unilateral bans, proclaimed unbeknownst to an unknown woman.

Was Antonio-Maria actually thinking about marriage? Nothing was less certain, but the community—with Pietro at the lead—was thinking for him and letting him know as much. Noisily.

o

We had a guitarist with us, an old man who hardly ever sang and who, owing to diminished musical ambitions and the very limits of the local musical system, tuned only the last three strings of his guitar. The three chords he played over and over were our acoustic world. He was always available and liked more than anything to come with us on such outings.

In the morning I would see him arrive with his guitar in his *motocarrozella* (the English equivalent of this pretty word is "carrier tricycle"); the enclosed driver's cabin left a little room for the guitar. All day long, at Pietro's request, the charming old man strummed his three chords, which were more than sufficient to accompany a song.

The goal of the serenade consisted less of making music than of making noise around the person of Antonio-Maria. We had brought a few bottles along from the fête. Other sonorous objects were found on the spot. We played and sang for rather a long time. Antonio-Maria did not want to get up.

On the other hand, to Pietro's great satisfaction all the windows on the square around the church began to light up. Men in unorthodox sleepwear, with big smiles and carrying flashlights, invited us in to have a drink. At three in the morning, the square was experiencing an uncommon nightlife.

Were we engaged in persuasion or witnessing evasion? In any case Antonio-Maria wasn't budging. While continuing to play, we tested his determination by slipping under his open window. The neighbors swelled our ranks. From up above, from what in the complete dark seemed to be a stairway, a few projectiles were hurled at us: seasonal vegetables and empty tin cans. Pietro, who for the time being was improvising *strofette* about our misfortunes, managed to climb to the second floor to make peace while we continued to play dance tunes and the neighbors shuffled out a few steps.

Antonio-Maria was suspected of being ill, until the moment when he finally came down in an outfit that was neither diurnal nor nocturnal: an undershirt and long underwear. He opened his refrigerator. *Porchetta,* cheese, and wine filled us up. We spoke of everything, except marriage and women. Pietro brought up the Berbers again and Antonio-Maria found himself transported without transition, and, moreover, without much surprise, from sleep to Morocco.

As for myself, I wanted to go from Morocco to sleep. It was, however, time to get up. The aroma of coffee invaded the square. I was intending to drive back that same day, or at least to go as far as a nearby pine forest where I could take a much-anticipated and belated nap.

o

It was very hard for me to formulate a coherent and truly documented account of my experiences in Thiesi. In Pietro's shadow I had done a little research; but twice I had lost my notes: the first time when we were with the fire watchmen contorting ourselves to contemplate the sky; and the second time during one of our nocturnal escapades, and I didn't even know where.

Interestingly, the musical traditions of Thiesi that had kept me close to Pietro were not really very rich. Under Pietro's guidance I sensed an energy of despair. Thiesi was going around in circles. It seemed those living in the town were attempting to regain a history that was being largely torn apart by a wave of emigration that had drained the land of its blood. Thiesi no longer had the music of its behaviors, nor even that of its intentions. The machine was running on empty. Except for our old guitarist the musicians whom I hastily met had trouble mustering the energy it took to rally round Pietro. They followed him with their eyes. Their smiles reflected acquiescence.

The young people sang, rather clumsily, gathering here and there what could be included in a now short-circuited culture. I was precisely one of

Pietro Nannu of Lodè with his family (1985).
Photo by Bernard Lortat-Jacob.

those gathered items. In my baggage I brought Moroccan stories, from the other side of the Mediterranean, and a knowledge of Sardinia that served to increase energies. I could just as easily have left my health there as Pietro, I believe, is leaving his own.

○

The thought of going back to Thiesi frightens me. I fear finding Pietro extinguished, worn out, and alcoholic. But I still ask about him when I'm passing through the area. It is possible to hear about Pietro everywhere in

Sardinia, since everyone seems to know him. I learned that he had lost his father and that his mother, in the days that followed, had become partially paralyzed because of the loss. My flight is therefore all the more natural, for it is becoming increasingly difficult to connect my joys to such pain.

IRGOLI

We were in France. Tonino was on the phone. I wondered about his tone of soft and discreet conviction. He was talking to his brother and trying to persuade him that they should meet in Montpellier where he was singing that same evening.

Tonino had come to France with some other villagers from Irgoli. He hadn't seen his brother Francesco in thirty years. Francesco lived in the south of France. Married to a Frenchwoman, he did not appear convinced that he should renew ties with a past he wanted to forget. He replied politely, declined the invitation, and did not seem to think it indispensable to continue on the subject. In any case his wife intervened; the conversation then turned to the accident of a son who had hurt himself on their tractor a week ago. In the span of a few seconds Tonino learned that his brother had a tractor, a son, and that the son had a knee, injured. He inquired about the knee with an almost medical interest; the knee of a nephew whom he had never seen. He understood at the same time that his brother would not be returning to Sardinia or to Irgoli. His repeated invitations would achieve nothing.

o

Irgoli, where Tonino lived, is the village I most enjoy visiting. In a certain way Irgoli is on the fringes of Sardinia. The harshness of the interior of the country is tempered there with a unique light and civility.

Throughout my travels in Sardinia, of all the places where I've been persuaded to extend my stay, Irgoli has been the most affectionate and the sweetest. The sea air, the very sweet wine from the almost Tuscan hills of the hinterland, the beauty of the girls there, their natural elegance, and even more, the way they effortlessly change from traditional costumes into little Benetton outfits, the great number of young people, and finally, the collective management of merrymaking all beckon me, almost despite myself, to Irgoli as soon as I arrive on the island. And I always stay there longer than is really necessary.

Tonino, talking on the phone as if he were at home, was the very picture of Irgoli's civility. He occupied a distinct place in the village: he was no longer one of the noisy young men and not yet one of the silent old men.

Tonino was fifty, maybe fifty-five years old: the ideal age for a singer; the voice is mature at that age, polished and relaxed; the emotion of youth seems entirely centered on the music. At this age musical forms are nourished on final exuberances. Tonino, like the rest of his generation, enjoyed the natural self-assurance of his status as a mature man and the certainty of being able to move his audience.

And yet he had nothing of the star about him; he was never seen to speak out of turn; he spoke in the manner of the songs he sung: each note, however ornamental it may have been, played a part in the whole fabric, although a technical and controlled "tremolo" might have hinted at a certain fragility.

Tonino's singing embodied and reflected Irgoli, somehow capturing the essence of its delightful climate, wine, and inhabitants. But it was never overly sweet. As clear, precise, and powerful as the image of all of Sardinia, it revealed an unshakable moral conviction.

In fact, the great charm of Sardinia lies in a balance between fragile tenderness and moral strength, as embodied in Tonino. On occasion I have wished that one of these qualities might exist without the other or, more precisely, that tenderness might win out over moral strength (this being more in line with my own natural tendencies). I now realize that the absence or weakness of the one is directly prejudicial to the existence of the other.

There is a third component to the Sardinian character relating to the rules of hospitality. These rules exist in Irgoli, but they do not have the imperative nature they do in Barbagia, in the country's interior. Assuming the form of a dense conviviality, they leave the guest a little freedom, so a visitor's life is particularly sweet there.

Some German girls were beginning to learn this; in the month of August they brought their suntan lotion to a country where the local boys were particularly attentive. But Tonino, an old bachelor, was not a "hunter" of German girls. The name of a woman has never been connected to Tonino, despite all the love songs he's known for.

o

Arriving unexpectedly each time, I don't ever remember seeing Irgoli not involved in a fête—whether one was just ending, or in full swing, or being prepared . . . Either a fête had taken place a few days earlier or one would take place in the next few days. In Irgoli little fêtes with a few friends in the "countryside" and big calendar or patron saint fêtes—both of the village and of neighboring villages—alternate and are combined, each time awakening enclaved communal spaces.

At the heart of these fêtes, which are normally very cheerful, I sensed, however, an automatic festiveness and moments of "make believe" that were foreign to what I knew of Sardinia. On several occasions—especially at small local fêtes—in spite of the wine, the singing, and the usual joking around—I had the impression that the spirit of the people participating rang false. These fêtes took the form of fastidious, more or less successful exercises hastily put into place. I now understand that people participated in them systematically quite simply so as not "to lose the hang of it." It was only a *prova,* as they say in Italian—that is, both a "trial" and a "rehearsal"—which was as necessary to a fête as it was to music.

Just as career soldiers daily prepare for war by embellishing strategies and fastidiously maintaining their weapons, each day saying to each other, "Ah! Today is the day!" the people of Irgoli seemed to fear that the village would fall asleep in an individualistic peace; thus they led a daily battle so that, with the help of a few ingredients such as wine, cheese, and *porchetta,* the community machine would not rust. And it sometimes happened—as we will see—that the *prove* did indeed result in true social shows.

In these collective festivities nothing was said about the need to be together. In this respect Tonino was within the norm. He was not the type to talk about what he was feeling, had felt, or could feel: when he wasn't singing he was usually silent, but his behavior couldn't be considered an entrenchment. Although silent, he was always present. Perhaps he knew that when the rules of the game were uttered, they disturbed or ruined the game itself.

It was, however, normal in Sardinia to resort to the explicit; but one is not told how things work. Everyone gives of himself, but without giving himself away, and without saying why he does so.

If one never speaks of the internal mechanism that establishes or maintains a network of social relationships, this is quite simply because it is obvious, automatic, and possibly ritualized. On the other hand, potentialities, mythical projections, and imaginary flights are normal; myth and speech sketch reality; it is up to the latter to conform.

One of the first developments of myth consists of self-parody: real life is thereby transposed, transcended by way of words. In every human society whose credo is not puritanism, he who makes people laugh always wins points. Attention is focused on the best storytellers, who target the little circle of villagers who happen to gather to listen or the wider social realm they represent.

At once a little theatre and a place for daily rehearsals, the "bar"—that is, the café—becomes the favored place for these mythical intrigues. New stagings are improvised there every day and, taking on the form of a fragmented tale, the *barzeletta*—a type of joke—becomes an epic.

The café is in itself the symbol of masculine leisure (women, at least on one side of the bar, are excluded from it). Besides snippets of news pertaining to everyday village life, each client brings in with him a personal variant to the imaginary scenarios concocted at the café. The owner serves as both witness and referee.

o

The bar is home to its own form of music known as "guitar song." Simple in its principles, performed following a regular pattern, this singing does more than extend communal relationships: it forms them. The guitarist strums a few chords, which provide the singers with the harmonic route they must follow. This is the first rule of the game. Each participant must do his best to follow along.

Guitar song. Irgoli (1993). Photo by Bernard Lortat-Jacob.

Standing around the guitarist, the singers take turns coming in. There are principles that dictate the distribution of singers, principles that cannot be ignored. The song turns and passes from one protagonist to another. The circle is closed when all the singers without exception have performed their *strofetta*. Then a new cycle begins.

Like the bar itself "guitar song" is a semiopen structure. When a new client appears he can join the group already formed, join in on one or two musical cycles, then leave the way he entered, as one would a conversation. But he can enter in only at his turn and can leave only once his turn is over. The rules of politeness are musical here, and are scrupulously observed. Alternation is the master word: each singer signals his readiness and in turn makes his presence known.

"Guitar song" is an almost daily social exercise but one that takes place primarily in the evening. One can then take the time to appreciate the variety of voices and styles. In "guitar song" collective strength is born out of an ordered display of the individuals present.

There is another type of singing practiced in Irgoli, this one polyphonic, in which musical expression is confined to a small, tightly formed chorus led by a soloist. This is the *a tenore*, or sustained, singing in which men do not take turns coming in but rather all come in at the same time. The exercise then consists of "forming a block" with the other singers and, by following the soloist, of blending one's voice into those of the others. *A tenore* singing rests on principles of massed sound. Led by singers like Tonino, it borders on the sublime: the cohesion of the group is strongly asserted. The chorus seems to close upon itself, drawing the sources of its expression from within. But *a tenore* singing is both too beautiful and too intense to adapt to the atmosphere of the bar. The musical form is not open and the number of singers, strictly limited to four, does not provide for any eccentric interventions. However, the pleasure of being together and an abundance of wine, much to the detriment of the musical results, sometimes cause those basic rules to be relaxed.

o

Singers who excel in the two styles are rare. Tonino was one of the few. He sang naturally in the bar when he was surrounded by close friends and, with his usual reserve, led the *a tenore* chorus when asked to. He went on singing trips with his friends when he could take time out from his farming, under exceptional circumstances that he could not refuse. They then would take the music of Irgoli outside the village and sometimes even outside Sardinia.

When someone went to ask Tonino to sing, he always made them beg, claiming he had too much work or was too tired. In point of fact, his hesitations could be attributed to his natural modesty.

o

In the region around Irgoli the public works department had launched some initiatives that year. The new road signs they put up were dark blue. They were replacing the old ones, which were considered useless by the people living in the area who had either torn the signs down or scribbled additional information on them in white paint each time the administration had forgotten a village on its list.

Another initiative, this time more serious, had been taken regarding the bridge that connected Irgoli to the main road. It had been abruptly closed to traffic. The village and the hinterland were suddenly isolated. No plan for a replacement had been proposed. The decision was harsh and unfair. It is true that the bridge was old, but trucks hauling enormous blocks of marble had been using it for what seemed like forever.

Moreover, it was suspected that behind this closure there was some scandal *à l'italienne,* some of those shady bribes that were a specialty of Christian Democrats, though not exclusively theirs.

To get to the village one had to improvise by taking a long and uncomfortable dirt road. I don't know whether it was out of embarrassment or negligence, but the public works department had not taken very much trouble to indicate the detour.

○

Upon our arrival three years ago the region was undergoing an unusual upheaval. The bridge (or rather the absence of a bridge) was mobilizing everyone. The village center, at which point several roads intersected, was completely filled with people. In greater numbers than usual men, women, and children were gathered together. The church bells rang. The loudspeakers of the festival committee were in place and this time they were not transmitting music. A microphone was passed from hand to hand. Men shoved each other in order to speak. The women stayed around them. Various officials of the province—in dark suits and ties—stood nearby. For the time being Irgoli was speaking. More or less well.

A professional unionist brought up the workers' struggle in an obscure speech using obscure language; a farmer took the microphone in turn and announced that he would speak in Italian, then, having spoken three words, switched definitively to Sardinian; a merchant complained of the backache he had developed from taking the detour every day. His weariness was equal to that of his car. Before letting the elected officials of the province speak, the mayor mentioned the incontestable competence of the engineers responsible for closing the bridge. The discussion could be summed up in these words: "*Questo ponte è un ostacolo!*" "Indeed, the bridge is an obstacle!"

Compared to the mayor's rhetoric, that of the provincial politicians was slick. They spoke numbers. The cost of rebuilding the bridge had an impressive number of zeros. As if they were talking about a familiar sum of money, each person gave his opinion on the amount with the ease of a housewife discussing the price of melons.

The Province promised. They would have to wait. There was no shortage of administrative details to vouch for the positive nature of that wait and the brilliance of the politicians' actions.

o

The demonstration drifted toward the river. The bridge then received its praises and Tonino was in the first row: people sang and danced on the bridge of Irgoli. They discussed its weaknesses while assessing its resistance to time. Masons, of which there were many in the village, proposed to reinforce it. Three cement mixers were placed on the side of the road. The bridge took on a new look if not a new solidity. But it remained closed and, in any case, the changes it underwent were illicit. Irgoli was gradually entering into illegality.

Barriers to the bridge, erected during the day, were torn down at night. *Carabinieri* (policemen) had to stand guard for entire weeks. With the good weather people came to have picnics around it; there was singing, guitar playing, and, of course, accordion music, which was always a part of picnics in Irgoli.

The three municipal guards were torn between the need to uphold the law and their desire to mix with the villagers demanding justice. After hesitating for a long time, and after weighing the risk he would take in breaking a law he was supposed to uphold, Franco opted for wearing two hats. Between night and day he changed his civil status. At night he took off his official cap to participate in the subversive acts of the others.

They resorted to explosives. The workers in the marble quarries on the outskirts of Irgoli knew how to use them. When the charges were detonated to break up the enormous boulders that the police had placed to block access to the bridge, the explosives at least had the merit of demonstrating that the structure was not as fragile as they had believed . . .

Positions hardened on both sides. Barriers were answered with barriers. The people of Irgoli set them up on the surrounding roads to extend the scandal to all of Baronia. Twenty people were arrested and sent to court. The villages involved in the bridge affair were now the ones with which the same fêtes were shared. The closed bridge affected Orosei, on the sea side, and Lula, on the mountain side.

The people of Irgoli always attend the fêtes of Nostra Signora del Rimedio in Orosei and those of San Francesco in Lula. Our Lady and Saint Francis collaborated and provided their commemorative strength; political solidarity quite naturally went hand in hand with the ritual system.

o

The bridge received new praise. People dedicated songs to it, which Tonino sang with the little chorus, without a guitar, given the seriousness of the situation. Questioning the competence of the technicians as well as the abruptness of the police intervention, Irgoli undertook its own scientific experiments. One fine day a truck weighing twenty tons loaded with blocks of marble braved the closure unbeknownst to the authorities. The driver was celebrated.

Provincial officials came many times to the site. They had at least to wrench the people of Irgoli from the hands of justice. They had a few concessions up their sleeves. One of them was particularly appreciated and discussed at length: only light cars would be permitted to cross. They then had only to adjust the entrance to the bridge with new blocks of marble in order to allow only Fiat 500s, 600s, and 127s to cross.

Rather quickly it was discovered that by careful maneuvering larger vehicles could also make it through the blocks, which were regularly inched apart so that little by little small trucks made inroads as well.

Vertical iron bars one-and-a-half meters high were placed along the entire length of the path, creating a narrow passageway: vertical bars turned into oblique ones; the security markers became "hedges of honor." From being continuously bent (toward the inside by the guards, toward the outside by the local residents), the iron markers finally gave way.

o

Plans were then made to design a new bridge. Upstream or downstream from the first? On the mountain side or the sea side? On the sea side there was Orosei and tourism; on the mountain side there was Nuoro, the big town, with its shops. Everyone voted for the side that concerned him most.

I followed the plans from time to time, but eventually the decision became less radical and more in line with custom: the new bridge would quite simply be built parallel to the old one, a few meters below it.

While waiting for the first stones to be placed, the bridge was the site of new fêtes, which were added to the calendar and patron saint fêtes.

With promises acquiring some reality and financing plans coming together, general performances gradually gave way to specific rehearsals: the fête once again became a "*prova.*"

The bridge enlarged the collection of communal experiences, but it did not constitute a feat of arms. At the Vacca bar or at Giuseppe's, it was talked about as a daily fact and as the normal continuation of a habitual exercise. But if the closing of the bridge had caused such a fury, it was because the decision of the public works department, even though technologically justified, was socially unacceptable. It authoritatively broke off the communal relationships that Irgoli had maintained forever with the town and with other villages in Baronia.

o

Three years after the first demonstrations against the closing of the bridge, the foundations for the new bridge were made official and Irgoli received the visit of leftist radicals who pompously saluted the popular victory of the people of Irgoli. Tonino was at the gatherings.

That evening a few *compagni,* Communists or bearded "Sardists" living on the continent, sang what they called "traditional songs"—political songs, in fact, clumsily performed, written in the usual style, with lyrics that were almost Albanian, and using musical chords reminiscent of both Boy Scout and Piedmont singing. They were artificially creating the outlines of a community that the community itself had never felt the need to draw. Tonino quietly nodded his head with an air of both understanding and surprise. It was *his* history that people were talking about. His smile, punctuated with regular emissions of "*Boh!*" could be taken as an acquiescence. He seemed happy that these young people who had come from so far away were speaking of a bridge that was so near.

The kind of attention he paid, noticeably distant and thus comparable in every way to that shown for the injured knee of his young nephew, reflected his natural transparency. Everything concerning other people was of interest to him, and nothing that he owned was truly his. Surely this was the reason why, swept along by a tradition that he endlessly transfigured, he was such a great singer.

But that evening, indifferent to verbal jousts on the subject of Sardinian culture and to neo-Scout songs that, in attempting to glorify that culture, succeeded only in denying its existence, Tonino did not sing. He had other concerns: the recent death of a young brother—a different one who lived in Sardinia—and the worrisome maintenance of gardens located far from the village that were suffering from the summer drought.

SANTU LUSSURGIU

THE WOMEN OF SANTU LUSSURGIU HAD STOPPED WHAT THEY WERE DOING TO TALK TO ME FOR A MOMENT ABOUT THE ADVENTURE OF THEIR CHRIST. THEY WERE DECORATING THE ALTAR OF THE LARGE CHURCH WITH DELICATE FLOWERS THAT WERE SOMEWHAT INCONGRUOUS WITH THE TRAGIC FUNERAL RITES THEY WERE PREPARING.

Maternal gestures and technical discussions were the natural prelude to the Easter ritual (this was Holy Thursday). In an intimacy that the church seemed to forbid, my intervention appeared abrupt. Thus the conversation suddenly broke off—my embarrassment brought it to a sudden close—and ended with a suggestion: I needed to go see Pietro Lombardini (*Maestro Pietro*, as the women called him); he knew everything that might interest me.

o

Pietro Lombardini was an old scholar who wore a cap and dark glasses; both shielded him from the discomfort of the sun. The dark glasses gave him the air of an intellectual fatigued by too much reading, while the flat cap worn by Northerners turned him into a villager.

Politicized in the Italian way and a great lover of popular art, he was, however, not entirely like the other residents of Santu Lussurgiu. They didn't need to be great lovers of anything to live a daily passion that was fed by their surroundings and, ultimately, by a common sense of things. As for Pietro, he always felt the need to distinguish history, the past, the present, myth, and the future.

He was a knowledgeable man whose notoriety rested on the fact that he was constantly sharing his educated opinions on the world in general and on Sardinia in particular, making erudite speeches that were not always extremely clear. But the quality of his syntax, and even more the strength of his delivery, was enough to make the difference. His notoriety inspired moderate benevolence. Pietro Lombardini knew more than other people, which, in a certain way, authorized him to do less than they did. It was as if the distance conferred by knowledge resulted in a visibly diminished taste for action. He took less pleasure in joining others and doing the same things in the same way. He seemed to have lost a facility for repetition and, as an experimenter, was primarily interested in observing how with no apparent weariness the same events and facts were reproduced on a daily basis.

He was interested in the past and had invited me to visit his museum on Sardinia. It was in a certain sense an anti-Sardinian museum, in that it included standard objects common to all Mediterranean civilizations and, indeed, in its very cultivation of archaism.

Archaism is not really part of the Sardinian mind. The distant past left behind the big round towers, the *nuraghi;* the recent past—that of the last few centuries—a few large, not too modest Italian buildings that are interesting only insofar as they are not annoying. They are at best buildings one lives next to. In most Sardinian villages one would search in vain for the *centro storico* that could contribute a few lines to the editor of a guide book. The true center of Sardinian villages is ahistorical and is used everyday, squeezed between the sides of roads and fed on uncompleted new construction.

Conversations with Lombardini had already touched on music, the avatars of the local industries—textiles and "cognac," which had once had its hour of glory—the technical wizardry of a hydraulic carding machine, and the relationship between the church and the religious brotherhoods. Given the hour, it seemed likely that we would end up at the local bar. The respective qualities of various wines had, moreover, already been mentioned several times throughout the morning. Pietro was going to go get a bottle, and that task would have been accomplished some time ago if we hadn't had to talk about everything. No doubt the heated nature of our conversations made one forget the appropriate automatic niceties.

o

It was then that three intruders made their appearance: a man flanked by two municipal guards. The man, who attracted everyone's attention and who, unlike the guards, did not belong to the local landscape, was quite elegant—he wore a light brown suit of contemporary cut that sported a whimsical addition: a somewhat asymmetrical bow tie verging on a neckscarf.

Sicily, and even more so a hint of Naples, apparently had left on him the mark of an urbanity that seemed elegant by dint of being natural. The two guards, next to him, looked almost sloppy.

The municipal guards of Sardinia, who are in a way the equivalent of French country policemen of the past, have recently begun to wear uniforms whose colors (white and black), cap (too big and too flat), shoulder straps, and silver-plated insignia highlight an official arbitrariness.

Midseason required them to wear sweaters underneath their jackets. These sweaters softened the lines of a uniform that was supposed to give the person wearing it the rigidity of an official function, if not an unfriendly demeanor. The dust of the road, the late hour of the morning, and stops in several bars had visibly rendered their spit and polish less fresh.

For the time being the guards on duty seemed engaged in a relation neither of surveillance nor of friendship. As for the man they accompanied, despite his Mediterranean air and a bearing that was as relaxed as it could be in spite of his elegance, he was obviously not from Sardinia. He was there—we quickly discovered—because he, too, wished to learn something about a history toward which he could only be directed by the *maestro*, Pietro Lombardini.

o

"You are French? I, too, am French," he told me right after we had been introduced.

I had to be convinced of that. He took an identification card from his pocket: "Dimitrius Onni," born in Tunis in 1925. The seal of the French Republic crowned it all. And yet it was still hard to believe.

Dimitrius's speech, when he spoke French, had inherited Italian syntax

83

and was heartily fed on borrowings from slang. His Italian appeared rather shaky; a few sentences in Sardinian came back to him in little bursts of words.

His parents were Sardinian, he tells us—from Santu Lussurgiu in fact. They had left the region in the prime of their lives, had had two children in Tunisia to whom they had spoken, in Sardinian, of their land. But he had essentially lost the use of his native tongue. A son of Santu Lussurgiu, he knew no one in the village and no one knew him. Dimitrius Onni had never set foot in his father's village, nor even in Sardinia. He had arrived on the island the day before and was planning to leave again the next day. He had come only "to see" and at sixty years old had wanted to discover a land he had heard about throughout his childhood, thus one he knew well, a land that was inseparable from his father's character (he never spoke of his mother). For him his father embodied Sardinia in its entirety. Indeed, he had come to the island especially so that people would tell him about his father, Salvatore.

Salvatore Onni had first emigrated to continental Italy then, owing to his antifascist attitude, had been exiled to Tunisia. The cruel treatment inflicted on the father, which went as far as torture, had bruised the son. Lucidly and without exaggeration, Dimitrius revisited these fragments of his past. A Holy Thursday story; time did not erase the injuries.

After the time they spent in exile, the family emigrated two more times: to Sicily and to France. And Dimitrius joined two apparently contradictory organizations: the Communist Party and the police force. The southern suburbs of Paris, a post where he ultimately served as an inspector, completed his education and provided him with a vocabulary that was both exotic and common.

His father had been at school with Gramsci. Gramsci in turn extended the mythical image of the father. With Pietro Lombardini leading the way, the first thing to do was to examine with a magnifying glass the photos of Gramsci piously preserved in the village. A photo was found, one that had been taken at school. It was a rather fuzzy group photo. Next to the author of *The Prison Notebooks* we looked for the father whose traits were unknown.

o

Kinship is above all a matter of memory in which the eldest are always in a privileged position. They know. And while an initial inventory of the Onni family was being drawn up, the old Onnis in the village, in flesh and blood, showed up with the hope of falling into the open arms of a forgotten cousin.

But before getting to that point, it was necessary to interview the various candidates for kinship on his father's side. The whole business became more complicated as the number of applicants grew. Moreover, there were notably few of the details needed to reconstruct a true history. The true history was in fact that of everyone. Everybody had a role in it to the point that Salvatore Onni's traits, instead of becoming clearer in the course of the inquiry became increasingly indistinct: apparently all those who bore the Onni name had done the same thing, had known the same misery; all had been shepherds, and nothing of what the Onni son believed to be unique to his father was truly so. He looked at the Old Men always posing in the same way in the yellowed photographs. They all looked alike.

In the course of things Dimitrius talked about himself, as if he had already understood that he was expected to do so in this land. As a footnote to his research, which asked only to be sidetracked, he pointed out how he had hesitated for a long time before undertaking his trip. In the end the recent death of his sister, who had never seen Sardinia either, made the decision for him. Bringing to a close a complicity based on a myth, her disappearance had the effect of stripping the myth of its raison d'être. That was what induced him to take the first step and thus to cross the sea. By way of Sicily.

For this trip Dimitrius and his wife, Irène (a Frenchwoman who from a first marriage had given birth to a famous jazz musician), had fitted out an old Volkswagen van they had bought from some English hippies.

Besides a return to his roots, Dimitrius's trip had another motive: dance. "Modern" dance, as they both called it—polkas, mazurkas, and waltzes—was a passion they shared. Dance halls served as milestones on their itineraries.

Whereas other people go to Italy to visit monuments or museums, they made the rounds of local dance halls, simply to dance in them, or perhaps to participate in competitions, happily competing with younger dancers. Competitions that they sometimes won. And in the little van piled high with mattresses and picnic paraphernalia, the dance costumes had a special place.

Taking off the mechanic's suit that he usually wore, Dimitrius put on his show costume, his dance costume, for his entrance into the village. His wife was in the shadows—I didn't even notice her when she came into the house of my friend the scholar. She disappeared just as discreetly in the late afternoon while Dimitrius was led from house to house and from street to street. She had settled into the van to wait for the end of his adventures, an end that was apparently nowhere in sight. Later Dimitrius joined his wife in the van and was visited by a few new Onnis who had been forgotten in the first round. He was consulted and henceforth took his role as historiographer quite seriously. The entire village was now mobilized to discover a common past. The van served as a dispensary, handing out declarations of memories. Everyone was eager to enter, extirpating something of himself, which Onni passed on to his next visitors. Everyone involved had put himself sixty years in the past, but the affair was a contemporary one; its only limit in time was the impending departure of the couple, for whom the idea of returning was already disturbing.

o

The evening of Holy Thursday was not an evening of dance for the Onni couple. Like everyone else, they went to church, where the wooden Christ with the tragic, olive-green face was put back on the cross as he was every year. Then the cross was raised up and carried in a procession through the streets of the village to a church nearby.

o

I mentioned to Dimitrius how beautiful the songs of Holy Week were (Madame Onni had naively asked me if I had come from France to rehearse the singers). No, I replied, on the contrary, I had come so that they might teach me something about their art.

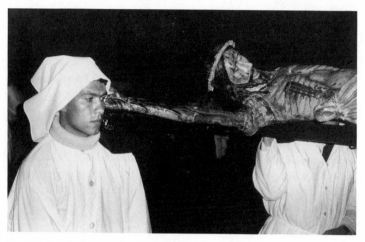

The Christ of Castelsardo. Holy Thursday. Castelsardo (1993).
Photo by Bernard Lortat-Jacob.

We had more than enough time to hear them. For Onni this was a Sardinian evening. The only one he spent on the island: the ferry had brought him the day before and would take him back home the next day.

o

The songs of Holy Week in Santu Lussurgiu have an incomparable power. They are sung by four men both in church and during the different processions that occur in the strangely silent night. Along with the cortege they displace many people. Christ, borne aloft on the cross, is held by the little choir, which assails him with harsh and painful harmonies at different locations dictated by the geography of the village. At the church, for his departure and return, the sound is full, abundant, reassuring. It assumes its aggressive quality outside, when the wind is blowing and it is hard to see anything at all. The large torches that are lit and carried for the occasion add to the fantastic atmosphere. Dimitrius was following the procession. During the day he had had a lot to drink, in proportion to his status as an important guest. The evening air slowly sobered him up as the mountain breezes brought their usual chill. Along the way he had lost his wife as well as his involvement in politics and unions, and his policeman's memories.

He stopped off at his van, parked in a lot below, where the choir had just recently stopped to sing. Among the tupperware, the piled-up dishes, the bath towels, and the dance costumes made of synthetic linen, he cleared a path for himself and fell asleep.

He left early the next morning. At dawn the van was no longer there. Yet Santu Lussurgiu is really not that far from the boat landing. But considering the effort it took to tear himself away from the area, he must have decided it was a good idea to leave before daybreak, before having to face the first entreaties of the village people to whom he had promised he would return and who had become his friends.

CASTELSARDO

SARDINIA

IN SANTU LUSSURGIU CHRIST IS OLIVE
GREEN; IN AIDO MAGGIORE HE IS THE
COLOR OF EARTH AND RESEMBLES AN AZ-
TEC DOLL: HIS BODY IS COVERED WITH HUMAN
SKIN GLUED ON WOOD AND HE HAS REAL HU-
MAN HAIR. THUS ARRANGED, HE LOOKS UN-
KEMPT, LIKE AN EMBALMED HIPPY, ALTHOUGH
HIS COLORING, BY CONTRAST, BRIGHTENS UP THE WREATHS OF FLOWERS
THAT SURROUND HIM. HIS HAIR EMPHASIZES THE SPIRITUAL DISORDER
THAT, FOR HUNDREDS OF YEARS, THE EASTER RITUAL HAS ATTEMPTED TO
DISCIPLINE.

The Christ of Castelsardo has put in his time. He has been carried
around the streets of the town so often, in the soft misty rain off the sea,
that after several centuries of good and loyal service, he has expired. And
this time for good. He has finally been laid to rest in the little church of
Santa Maria. He is replaced by another Christ, less handsome, but lighter
and easier to move around for the big processions of Holy Week.

o

Processions are the responsibility of the Santa Croce brotherhood, an
association of laymen, craftsmen, shop workers, masons, and fishermen.
And to insure that they proceed as they should through the town, the
prior, as a temporal substitute for Christ, meticulously chooses from
among the brotherhood the twelve apostles of Holy Week.

Twelve apostles—that is, twelve singers—following the dictates of
symbolism and arithmetic, are grouped into three choirs of four members
each. These are the three *cuncordos* of Easter whose voices, harmonically
ranged from low to high, are the *bassu*, the *contra*, the *boghi* (that is, "the
voice"), and the *falsittu*. There is no Judas.

o

Elected for the year, the prior is responsible for organizing the entire festival, and as regards the music, must reconcile two contradictory demands: he must select the twelve singers from among the candidates for the ritual, and if possible avoid offending the others through maladroit omissions.

An alert prior knows this well: to participate in an Easter choir is an honor and a momentous occasion in a man's life; but there are few who excel in all the repertoires and who are worthy, in the final analysis, of what they are to celebrate.

Thus the prior assembles his Holy Week the way a hostess arranges her dinner table for company: sometimes he favors an old man from a family of former brotherhood members, sometimes a younger man whose only wish is to assert himself, and sometimes a friend to whom he will offer the steep streets of the town for a few hours so that others can hear him sing.

It is in this way that every singer has had *his* Passion: the one in which he excelled in 1958, the one during which he made two or three false starts in 1963, and the one that, by singing too fast, he garbled a few years later. Everyone remembers.

o

Indeed, that year the prior had taken some risks. For the *Miserere*, he had chosen an old "lazzarone," Franco Flores. Tradition justified his choice; Franco embodied an ancient style, slow and solemn, that had become obsolete in modern times.

But old Franco, who was as ancient as his style, had not been active in the brotherhood for a long time: he had lost his taste for singing, if not for wine. Living alone, he spent most of his retirement at Gaston's bar; with Gaston he always found a patient, if not attentive, ear. In fact, when the prior invited him to sing, though many had heard him talk, no one had heard him sing for a long time.

I sat in on the first rehearsals, which began at Lent each year. Lent is the period for preparing voices more than it is one of abstinence. For forty days members of the brotherhood meet several times a week in the chapel of Santa Maria to practice their singing. They settle down in the choir of the little church and, using the altar, which is transformed into a picnic table and a bar counter for the occasion, spread out some food and a huge bottle of wine, which they consume during the evening. This is where they spend hours working on the difficult passages: the "Dolorosa" of the *Stabat Mater,* the "Misericordiam" of the *Miserere,* the "Exhaudi" of the *Jesu.*

Old Franco's voice was still beautiful, warm, and even more lyrical than expected. But, like the singer himself, the verses of the Psalm had lost much of their Latin. To the extent that he recalled the ancient words, they were full of uncommon sound combinations, but beyond what he remembered, they were drowned in the music and had become completely Sardinian. His singing had a lot of volume, but at the heart of Franco's inventive melodic proliferations, his choirmates, who were nevertheless experienced, had trouble finding their cues.

During such evenings of rehearsal and, in general, when preparing for any communal musical event, there is often an initial moment of anxiety when things do not fall easily into place. The product of an agreement that, like an act of love, must each time be re-created, harmony is formed gradually: from listening to the others and from controlling one's own voice come the first moments of satisfaction. But in the end these moments of grace and work do not last very long: tempers rise with the amount of wine consumed and the singing soon gets out of hand. Franco, who was drinking a lot, thus went without transition from a stupor he attempted to dispel with the help of his companions to an excitation that, given his level of blood alcohol, he was unable to control.

o

As one might expect, the Easter ritual leaves little room for carelessness. Limited in time, it occupies a rigorously measured space. As is clear from Holy Monday's large procession, nothing is more foreign to its aesthetic than wanton excess.

The procession begins at the little church of Santa Maria and after going up and down the streets of the town, ends three hours later at the cathedral located some hundred meters away. The mysteries, that is, the symbols of the Passion and the instruments of the torture Christ endures, pass by like a succession of mute scenes: the chalice, the crown of thorns, the chain and the rope, the spear, and so on. Held completely motionless, they are carried at arm's length by men whose faces are covered with cowls.

The three choirs are placed in fixed positions within the narrow processional line while, unaware of each other and separated by a great distance, the twelve mysteries of the Passion spread out in the town. The whole participates in an aesthetic of contrast: masks contrast with uncovered faces, the standing stations alternate with walking, and the brothers in white albs stand out in the night as does the music in the silence.

As a secular event the procession is a stage race: each choir takes its turn stopping in front of the houses that are to be honored. But it is also a race against the clock, the reverse of the kind practiced, for example, by the Tour de France, for here it is a matter of going slowly: each choir must force the one behind it to slow down and to increase the number of times it stops—in short, to sing a lot and for a long time. Contrary to appearances, the position of the first choir is not entirely advantageous, for if its members are unlucky enough to go too quickly, it is always possible for the others to arrive at the cathedral much later, emphasizing to all in attendance that there has been some precipitation on the part of the first.

o

That Monday it was raining and old Franco had hurried toward the cathedral where in the end each person was happy to find shelter from the dark, the rain, the wind, and the dampness of the evening. Not only had he urged his companions not to stop at the places where they were supposed to, but he had systematically omitted doubling the verses of the *Miserere*. The circuit of the town had been completed in less than three hours and the singers got back to the church early.

The second choir, singing the *Stabat*, did much better; it arrived quite late at the large, reassuring cathedral, where suddenly the sound of the choirs' music brightened in the full and sonorous acoustics. Throughout the whole procession the second choir had slowed down its singing to the point of blocking the *Jesu* choir. This third choir ultimately had to resort to standing still in the street without singing—which with customary irony everyone noted.

o

Miserere, Stabat Mater, Jesu: these three sacred texts, expressed diversely by the music, are part of an ordered theatrics. Opening the march, the *Miserere* is the expression of an age-old remorse concealed in the low voices of the choir. More lyrical and languid, the *Stabat* develops its two verses in a long lament in which the singers need to prolong the silences in order to catch their breath. It conveys the pain of a mother who has lost her son—a pain always present in a land of vendettas.

Closing the procession and standing near the crucifix held by the priest, the final choir, that of the *Jesu,* blends remorse and lamentation and brings the hope of redemption.

o

The next day there was a large crowd at Gaston's bar. Everyone had exchanged his white alb for his everyday clothes. Angelo, the bass for the *Stabat,* as portly as his voice, was wearing his mason's garb; Franco, the old lazzarone, standing proudly erect, was in a suit, vest, tie, and polished shoes. Released from his role, and thus completely self-confident now, he was crooning Neapolitan songs while gesturing an imagined guitar accompaniment. Other members of the brotherhood, having taken time off for Holy Week, had brought their children with them. They were all holding ice cream cones in their hands, thereby justifying their presence in the bar with their fathers.

They talked about the mishaps of the day before and attributed them to whoever had not yet arrived in the bar, and even more eagerly to the rigors of the climate. There was a demand for perfection in the singing and in the way it was carried out that was no doubt tied to its spiritual function. To be firmly established the perfection in the singing needed witnesses. Tradition then had names: there was Antonello the mason, whose powerful and full bass voice immediately reassured those at his sides; there was Balsano the fisherman, an expert on the customs of the land; or

Giovanni, the soloist whose shyness disappeared only when he sang: "I can only sing," he said, "I cannot speak."

The tape recorder was on the table. It, too, bore witness: engraving and aggravating mistakes, quite often it accused. Aware of the cohesion of the whole, each one listened to his part.

That cohesion—as I learned incidentally—has an objective feature; that is, it has the strange ability to manifest its existence acoustically. But for it to do so the four voices of the choir must be in perfect harmony. At that point a fifth voice, sung by no one in particular, makes its appearance in the upper register. It is called the *quintina* (literally the "little fifth") and is born of the harmonic fusion of the four real voices. Produced by the tight overlapping of the four consonant parts, the *quintina* testifies to the harmony of the singers and, as soon as they have made it "come out"— this is the goal the singers set themselves—it is present to the point of becoming overwhelming. One's musical attention does not tire of this acoustical wonder while all the efforts of the singers join together to reveal it. Performed in this way, the song is no longer choral but a lied, borne aloft by the voices of the men. The "Dolorosa" in the *Stabat Mater* then takes on the quality of a long woman's lament. For the *quintina* is a woman: the word's gender shows this, but so too, and even more so, does the voice's light and airy timbre, contrasting with that of the powerful male voices that produce it.

A phenomenon of harmonic fusion, the *quintina* is born of the chord that engenders it. It is the acoustical proof of perfect harmony, and it is for that reason that the choir is called "concord" (*cuncordu* in Sardinian).

Because it testifies to and at the same time reveals the perfection of the singing, the *quintina* is of a spiritual essence: like the masked faces of the Passion, it is hidden behind appearance and, significantly, presents itself as the acoustic attribute of the ineffable.

Gathered around the tape player, the singers claimed to hear it more or less well. The *quintina* hides behind vowels and consonants and takes on a different coloring depending on the nature of the harmony. It finally slips away when one thinks one has it; but, unwitting disciples of Pascal that they were, the best singers would not have been looking for it if they hadn't already found it.

However, the conversation could probe no further into the mystery. The social force that caused the *quintina* to emerge is obscure, as were the commentaries to which it gave rise; while the tape was playing, old Franco was in Naples and Gaston, calling one and all to witness, initiated a conversation on the quality of the ice cream he made.

o

The business of Holy Week and that of everyday life elicit the same attention. Gaston convinced everyone that his ice cream was worthy of any other; little cups of it passed from hand to hand through the bar. First he gave out his ice cream, then that of the *concorrenza* (the competition). The competition came from the shop across the street, immodestly called "The Ice Cream Maker."

Gaston's regular customers wondered about the use of the definite article. Does someone who makes ice cream have the right to call himself "the" ice cream maker if he is not the only one to make it? asked Giuseppe. For an entire hour a discussion was pursued on the properties, either ideal or claimed, of ice cream and cookies, about which no one claimed to know anything—such concerns were for women and children—and which were subjects good above all as fodder for rhetorical games.

It was thus that one proceeded to distinguish the structure of the ice cream (*la struttura del gelato*), its appearance, and its consistency before approaching the problem from the other end: by way of a bar owner's relationship with his clientele and, in the end, Gaston's relationship with his own clients. The clarity of the discourse benefited from the levity of the subject.

The rhetoric in question, in large part Latin, as it happens, is organized in an always expansive intellectual space that is fitted out with familiar tools. Before formulating a sentence and even before giving it meaning, "On the one hand" and "on the other hand," "on one side" and "on the other" are used. Without for all that coming to any conclusions. Negations and "howevers" go back and forth with the regularity of a pendulum, most often ending in an "*ormai!*" or a doubtful "*boh!*" (which might be translated as "so!"), leaving the door open for subsequent investigations.

Procession on Holy Thursday. Castelsardo (1990).
Photo by Bachisio Masia.

Quite often this art of discourse, learned in early childhood, condenses meanings to the point of confusing opposites: "It is not that water scares me, but I fear it"—this statement, which a little girl might say at the seashore to her *genitori* (parents) who are watching her from the beach, verges on nonsense; but it is only an exaggerated form of what Cocco had said a few weeks earlier on the boat: he "liked poetry, but not music." He spoke from experience, knowing as well as I did that in Sardinia as elsewhere the one rarely went without the other.

It is thus that the brotherhood of Santa Croce devoted itself sometimes to singing and sometimes to discourse; the members, like hunters lying in wait, track down all possible subjects in order to circumvent their meaning: the bistro tables and especially Gaston's bar counter serve as training grounds for more important things—like processions.

The thinking spaces and the processional routes of Castelsardo are fitted out in the manner of great treasure hunts whose rules are regularly rediscussed and in which everyone has a role. The alternating form of the singing in turn prolongs the dialectics.

Giovanni practices singing, Giuseppe verbalizes. It is thus that at the bar and in church the brotherhood of Santa Croce plays interminable games of which they are both the objects and the rule makers.

And yet the goal is simple: it is a matter of sharing the most meaning possible. And insofar as the act of sharing is part of the meaning, this requires time. But in Castelsardo—as everyone knows—it is the price one must pay so that out of the singing of masons, old retirees, and peasant members of the brotherhood the *quintine* emerge, and in the great nocturnal processions the Christs on their crosses each year are born anew.

AGGIUS

OF ALL FORMS OF MUSIC THE NEAPOL-
ITAN BEL CANTO IS THE ONE THAT DEAF-
MUTES CAN BEST APPRECIATE: PASSION,
LOVE, AND DRAMA ARE ARDENTLY EXPRESSED
IN IT. THE EMPHASIS ON EXPRESSION CAUSES
THE MUSICAL SYSTEM TO LOSE A GOOD NUMBER
OF ITS CONVENTIONAL PROPERTIES. THE
SINGER WANTONLY FATTENS THE MUSICAL FIGURES IN ORDER TO GIVE
THEM A HUMAN AND TRAGIC ALLURE. HE IS A MARTYR WE SEE SUFFERING,
A HERMIT IN ECSTASY, A LOVER WHO LANGUISHES. TO GIVE IT MEANING
NOTHING CAN BE NEGLECTED: THE MUSICAL EXERCISE IS A VAST META-
PHOR OF THE SOUL IN WHICH THE WHOLE BODY IS CALLED UPON.

○

When he sang "*Ah! che bell'aria fresca!*" Carlo Cicilloni was entirely
at ease. Each note was given expressive weight and was accompanied by
an appropriate gesture. Actor Louis de Funes could have been his father
and cartoon primadonna La Castafiore his mother. From the former he
inherited a plethora of passionate expressions, and from the latter a vocal
rhetoric that, well beyond the articulation of the larynx, governs the
mouth, the arms, the hands, the eyes, and the very posture of the body.

Born seventy-one years ago in Aggius, Carlo Cicilloni was Sardinian.
But he had learned how to sing in Rome; first by taking private lessons
with a master, then at the conservatory. His musical talents had caught
the attention of a gendarme from Aggius stationed in Rome who had
grown enamored of bel canto and had pushed him in that direction.

The Neapolitan bel canto does not, however, conceal anything original: academicism is always involved. The text, which includes several ad-

jectives per sentence as well as a full complement of clichés that shelter the listener from any surprises, makes the message obvious. It is an art of redundancy that, because it uses every means to display its charms, is always a bit cloying. As its name indicates, it claims to be beautiful; the singer believes it natural to accede to the sublime, and he must have a certain talent for combining sentimental narcissism with the unbridled outpourings of the heart.

○

Nothing is more foreign to Sardinian aesthetics than the art of the bel canto, which exaggeratedly favors individual expression and delights in a climate of immodesty. The oiled voices of the *cantatori* always make one smile and the bombastic gesturing expresses only ineptitude.

Through their apparently natural reserve, which undoubtedly obeys a secret order, the shepherds and peasants of Sardinia are sheltered from the destructive excesses of the soul. Important factors, which touch upon the social system, push them to refuse that which touches upon the intimate: a dense conviviality, the necessity of a daily mutual aid, and, in the end, an all-pervasive communal energy invite them to recognize themselves in other artistic expressions: in the collective dancing and the combined polyphonies of Barbagia, at the heart of the region.

Carlo had sung in church beginning at a very young age: at Christmas, Easter, and for Sunday high masses; more rarely in bars and in the village square. He had been initiated into the harmonies of polyphonic singing in four or five parts, and the church, which, in northern Sardinia, played an important role in the training of popular styles, had provided him with the first rudiments of a cultivated art.

In Rome he had acquired what people usually call a "voice." Before, he had sung in the Sardinian style in a narrow tessitura and with nasal intonation. The singing school had made his voice clearer, had rounded it out, had given it a power and a smoothness that, at the beginning, he did not know he had in him. In school he had learned how to make consonants ring, how exaggeratedly to color vowels, and, with the mastery of musical theory—he knew his two "Bona" by heart—had acquired a status as singer that enabled him to perform Massenet's *Manon,* Thomas's

Mignon, and the arias of a few great Verdian heroes, notably in the Teatro di Terracina.

But the sol-fa system is something quite different from a simple technique; it revolutionized the very conception of music for Carlo. In the traditional repertoire—that of his youth—the words fold themselves into the song in a narrow tessitura and join with the natural breath of the singer. Sol-fa, however, signals the notes, that is, the conventional units, which are carefully separated from each other. A specific expressive value must be attributed to each one of them according to a written text.

Compared with the milieu and customs he grew up with, that stay in Rome, which ultimately lasted some fifteen years, was an abrupt rupture. In Rome singing was no longer an exercise of solidarity among friends intended to enliven patron saint fêtes and Sunday masses. Its objective and raison d'être were no longer an effect of sheer numbers and, compared with the time when each person could sing as he wished provided he didn't overwhelm the others, everything had changed.

Based on an ascetic self-discipline, his Roman experience had given him the right to frequent patrician wealth. He had studied with Maestro Pescia, together with the daughter of the governor of the Bank of Italy, and during his initiatory training had encountered doctors and ministers.

Beyond a list of celebrities, which, moreover, he recalled with the speed of a vendor reading clauses guaranteeing the quality of his product, Carlo maintained few precise memories. From his moments of glory, which extended from his youth to the 1950s, he remembered above all his desire to escape the air of the city and his yearning for the countryside. Indeed, he fell ill at that time and remained physically drained for several years by life in the city.

o

Carlo was a peasant. He had been one once and had become one again. Each time I went to Aggius unannounced he was at work or in contemplation, as if planted in front of his grapevines. He approached his garden with the attitude of an interpreter as well as a stage director. When he trimmed a branch or made a cutting he stepped back the way a painter would who regularly distances himself from his canvas to grasp the tonality of the whole. He talked about the beauty of the nature that inspired his acts, borrowing images from the repertoire of lyrical songs. Operetta, opera, and the Neapolitan song had not undermined his know-how. Rather they guided his behavior and gave direction to his metaphors: the *"puro e sereno"* air suited the olive trees and the wine was as mysterious as the heart of a woman. The hills of Aggius enabled him to exercise his art to perfection: his wine is some of the best I have ever tasted in Sardinia.

o

Carlo had an obsession: to marry his Roman and Sardinian experiences and to see to it that the song of the land benefited from his knowledge of bel canto. Rome had not caused him to forget the songs of his childhood, which, during his exile, had fed his yearning. His plan consisted of reshaping them with the help of lyrical art.

Concerning Sardinian music he had a theory inherited from the contradictory concepts of those who had taught him the history of music in Rome. It had been brought to Sardinia by the Arabs, the Benedictines, and the Byzantines; but it was beautiful, ancient, profound, and ultimately original in the first sense of the word. In short, it had the characteristic of being both specifically Sardinian and completely imported. Born of a lost paradise, it had been preserved by shepherds who denatured its meaning by interpreting it with the voices of animals. He imitated their way of singing—*"Beng, Beng, Buong!"*—in a nasal voice and with gestures of disgust. Then he showed how it should be done and, raising his hand to place it next to his mouth, in the voice of Tino Rossi, repeated, *"Bheehi, Bhiihi, Bhoohh!"* In this way the Sardinian song in his opinion rediscovered its original distinction.

In fact, this attitude toward nasalization (judged to be vulgar whereas, beautiful and controlled, it can reinforce the superior harmonics and increase the possibilities of musical expression with a great economy of means) runs through and rules all lyrical art: nasalization is used, in Mozart for example, to express irony, but more generally, serves to mark the grotesque. There could thus be no question of rehabilitating the Sardinian song without banishing nasalization and, beyond that, without impeaching the aesthetics of the traditional song.

o

Evidently, Carlo could not conceive of teaching singing outside an institution. He had therefore created what he called a "school." In fact, as far as schools were concerned, it was quite simply a question of a high school that had been put at his disposal by a neighboring town for the rehearsals of the little choral group he led.

So the school was located in Perfugas, in Anglona. Perhaps because no man is a prophet in his own land. But especially for political reasons. Indeed Aggius had entered into the musical history of Sardinia by consecrating another of its singers: Galletto, a militant Communist, a friend of Dario Fo's, and the symbol of a popular expression that in his time bore the hopes of the Italian left. Although they were neighbors, Galletto and Carlo had never actually met. They sang the same songs, but not for the same audience or at the same fêtes. Carlo was favored by Christian Democratic municipalities; Galletto, until his recent death, was the exclusive singer at Communist Party fêtes.

o

Carlo and his group got together every Friday. Invited to judge on the basis of the evidence, I was to pick him up at his house and we would leave together.

At seven in the evening on Friday he was ready. He just had to put on his sunglasses and a cloth hat, one selected from his rich collection and that gave him the deliberate look of a man from the city. On the way, he expressed himself with all his authority as a maestro. He directed my driving and, when we got to Perfugas, I noted the respect he was shown: he was greeted with honor, flattered, shown attentiveness; people blushed when they spoke to him.

o

Carlo's flock was not yet assembled; they were scattered about enjoying the *passeggiata,* the evening stroll, and slowly joined us, one after another. A merchant, three artisans, a rich landowner, a rather self-assured teacher, and finally a shepherd from Anglona—all mature men—made up the choir. The school was closed for vacation and we had to take refuge in someone's home. On the way there we spoke of "traditional music" as one would a sick person whom one had to take good care of. Using the term "traditional" in this context suggested a conception of a culture that one no longer knew how to live or how to make live. As a general rule the term is used by those who participate in the culture secondhand, behind the ramparts of official knowledge and under the guidance of an authority in the matter.

A cold and somewhat scanty dinner—not truly Sardinian—awaited us. The culinary traditions conformed to what the music would be— basically a hybrid and partially sterilized. A little Pianola gave the tonic and chord progressions that would provide the harmonic base for the choir. The polyphonic parts were doubled. The mass effect sought after by those in the choir and the lack of elegance, visible in their demeanor, drowned the delicacy of the harmonies in a heavy consonance.

The repertoire was traditional; the manner of singing it was not. Carlo provided nuances of intensity with the gestures of an orchestra conductor. Each singer, in a certain sense stripped of responsibility, sought in Carlo's glance both security and confirmation that his singing was acceptable. As the leader, Carlo told each member of the group what he was to do and exercised his paternal authority. There were few pauses during the evening: caesuras were taken up by voluble explanations affirming his know-how.

While I attempted to record the session the recorder broke down. I was actually relieved. Nothing displeases me more than recording music I don't like; it provokes a strong disgust. By accompanying my pleasures, the tape recorder must have become a second stomach for me; it assimilates only the good and rejects the bad. When poorly executed, that is, produced and received without great emotion, music resembles lovemaking without love; it produces the same loathing.

We were not dealing with a technical problem; the singers had good voices, full and thick, and the polyphonic parts were in place. But music thus thwarted, surrendered to the power of an expert (even an enthusiastic one), loses its original meaning.

o

I remember precisely now what was at the origin of my love for Sardinian music; it was in France during one of the many fêtes devoted to the Mediterranean, when a group of singers and dancers from Barbagia performed: they all carried the strength of their culture within them, all the while appearing to excuse themselves for having it. "You see, I'm doing well, but I don't know why!" Contrasting with the gift of self that this music demanded, the singers' economy of gesture and their fear of performing created what is known as a balance—which is to say, something that is always just about to break apart. Conviction combined in that performance with fragility. Had the balance been upset, the song would have swayed either into the realm of the unaccomplished or into conformity.

o

His career having comforted him with certitudes, Carlo had opted for conformity. Music was considered beautiful and followed an exogenous model.

In a manner independent of the kindliness that emanated from his person, of his natural warmth, of a sense of conviction quite capable of sweeping along the least self-assured energies, Carlo re-created the relationships that he had learned in Rome. But while the choir was absorbed in him, he looked elsewhere. Toward the *palco scenico* (the stage), and more specifically toward a now mythical audience, seated and elegant, whose numerous testimonies he preserved in his mind.

The Emerald Coast, at the north of the island, where luxury tourism had developed, now formed his promised land; but he sought just as much, if not more, recognition in the heart of his Sardinian audience. Although he had preserved few tangible memories of his Roman career, he derived great pride from the awards hanging on the walls of his home, and from the trophies displayed on a shelf, which he had won with his choir in Sardinian folklore competitions.

In his relationship with Rome Carlo's position was that of an émigré. He had acquired a moral and professional capital there that he intended for his homeland, much as Moroccans, Portuguese, or Turks put aside their earnings in order to buy land or a business when they return home.

Paradoxically, his true career began in Aggius when he decided in the 1950s to train singers to make use of his knowledge and, in his own words, to return some nobility to Sardinian singing. This activity was not very lucrative, but it brought him a renown and a glory that were more real than those acquired in Rome. In his eyes his hope of being both a singer and a Sardinian was being fully realized.

o

Work being organized and limited in time, Carlo interrupted the rehearsal at exactly eleven o'clock. His disciples wanted to go to the bar (the desire to prolong the evening's relationships as long as possible was part of the usual rules of sociability). He came along with us without much enthusiasm. The practice of music must banish all excess. He himself did not drink, not even his excellent wine. His ascetic behavior was in strong contrast to the sweet convivial abandon that followed its course now that the rehearsal was finished.

We returned to Aggius relatively early in the night. With his usual enthusiasm Carlo spoke of music while recalling his role as *maestro*. In spite of their age and their corpulence, those whom he called his pupils were only children, and it was his mission, in the name of great art, to lead them with a firm hand. The music and the perfection to which he aspired were combined; they formed the very object of his rigorous training and self-discipline: therefore nothing made him suffer more than carelessness.

That evening I was accompanied by Francesco, a friend from Rome, and by my daughter Jeanne, whom he reproached for smoking (cigarette smoke is incompatible with the scent and the image of a woman). As we dropped him off he invited us to return, but with a new car, he stressed. It is true that my car, which for eight years had gone on all my Sardinian tours, had literally broken apart on the little country roads. I sensed that this would be its last trip.

SASSARI

THE EMPLOYEES IN THE TRAVEL AGEN-
CIES WERE SMILING: THE SUMMER SEASON
WAS ENDING AND THEY HAD NO MORE
SPACE TO SELL, EITHER ON THE BOATS FROM
OLBIA, OR ON THOSE FROM PORTO TORRES, OR
ON THE ALISARDA PLANES.

GOING BY WAY OF CORSICA IS AN ADVEN-
TURE THAT FEW SARDINIANS ADVISE. THE WELCOME IN BONIFACIO IS
SUMMED UP IN THESE TWO WORDS WRITTEN IN THICK LETTERS IN RED
PAINT AT THE ENTRANCE TO THE PORT: "*SARDI FORI!*" ("SARDINIANS, GO
HOME!").

o

The employee's smile was not that of the salaried worker happy to be
finished with his work. Rather it conveyed an invitation to an extended
period of hospitality. Whether or not this was against the will of that hospitality's recipient was not the issue—the traveler's nonfreedom went
without saying—it was measured by the affective and material investment
of the one who was hosting. The contract of hospitality is above all obligatory; it legalizes the alienation of guests. In short, for technical as well as
moral reasons, my opinion on my need to return to France bore little
weight.

The smile in question was that of the garage owner whom I had
troubled a short while before in his home while he was eating and who
had invited me to lunch, then to take a nap in his living room while he
took his with his kids on the big double bed in his bedroom. It was the
same smile he'd had that evening when the car had been fixed and yet he
still wanted me to stay for dinner and spend the night.

106

But for the Tirrenia employee, that insistent smile was also a veiled invitation to compromise. With an air of saying, "Ah! you wanted to come; and now you must pay the price!" it discreetly affirmed my nonright to indifference and recalled that insularity, isolation, and its difficulties are shared like everything else.

o

Only Sardinian emigrants trapped in their work and tourists, as organized as their trips, renounce from day to day this sharing of common things: at the shipyards of La Ciotat in France or in the mines of the Ruhr valley in Germany, the former pay dearly for having renounced it, while in a bay of Stintino the color of emeralds, the latter take the time to escape it in the early morning, windsurfing freely on the sea.

OTHER WORKS BY BERNARD LORTAT-JACOB

BOOKS

1980   *Musique et fêtes au Haut-Atlas.* Mouton-Ehess/Société française de musicologie.

1978   (With H. Jouad) *La saison des fêtes dans une vallée du Haute-Atlas.* Le Seuil.

1987   *L'improvisation dans les musiques de tradition orale* (compilation, including three chapters by the author and a cassette). SELAF.

        Jeu musical, jeu social: Une approche ethnomusicologique de l'aire méditerranéenne. Thèse d'Etat, Université de Paris X-Nanterre.

1991   *L'ordre intime des choses.* Julliard.

In prepa-ration   *Musiques en fête.* Université de Paris X/Société française d'ethnomusicologie.

        Les clochards célestes: Chroniques musicales de la Sierra Madre

        Chants de la Passion.

ARTICLES

1981   Community Music and the Rise of Professionalism, a Sardinian example. *Ethnomusicology* 25(2):185–97

        Danse de Sardaigne: composition, renouvellement: Ethnomusicologie et représentation de la musique. Edited by G. Rouget. *Le courrier du CNRS* 42: 42–43.

1982   (With Fr. Giannattasio) L'improvvisazione nells musica sarda, Due modelli. *Culture musicali* (Quaderni della Società di etnomusicologia) 1 (1): 3–35.

        Theory and "Bricolage": Attilio Cannargiu's Temperament. *Yearbook for Traditional Music* 14: 45–54.

        Improvisation et modèle; Le Chant à guitare sarde (with record). *L'Homme* 24(1): 65–89.

        Music and Complex Societies: Control and Management of Musical Production. *Yearbook for Traditional Music* 16: 19–33.

1986   Méthodes d'analyse en ethnomusicologie. *International Review of the Aesthetics and Sociology for Music* 17: 239–57.

        Le prix de la musique: Chronique sarde. *Modal, la Revue des musiciens routiniers* 3: 28–32.

1989   Penser l'improvisation. *Analyse musicale* 14: 15–18.

1990   Pouvoir la chanter, savoir en parler: Chants de la passion en Sardaigne. *Cahiers des musiques traditionnelles* 3: 5–22.

1993   En accord: Polyphonies de Sardaigne—quatre voix qui n'en font qu'une. *Cahiers des musiques traditionnelles* 6: 69–86.

RECORDS, COMPACT DISKS, AND FILM

1981   Polyphonies de Sardaigne. CD Collection CNRS/Musée de l'Homme, Le Chant du Monde LDX 74760 (Grand Prix du disque, Académie Charles Cros, 1982). Reissued as Compact disk, 1992 sous référence 274760.

1982   Sardegna 1, Organetto. Record, 30 cm/33 t. (with printed materials produced in collaboration with Fr. Giannattasio). "I Suoni" series, Cetra SU 5007.)

1984   Sardaigne, Launeddas. Collection Ocora/Radio-France, 558611.

1992   Sardaigne: Polyphonies de la Semaine Sainte. CD, Collection CNRS/Musée de l'Homme, Le Chant du Monde LDX 274936.

1990   Musica Sarda. Seventy-minute film produced by G. Luneau. Tara Production et la SEPT.

CONTENTS OF THE COMPACT DISC

Music of Sardinia

Recordings: Bernard Lortat-Jacob
Master tape: Jean Schwarz at the Ethnomusicology Laboratory of the Musée de l'Homme, Paris

1.	*A tenore* song	7:06
2.	*A tenore* song	3:10
3.	*A tenore* song	2:51
4.	*Ballu brincu*	6:30
5.	*Launeddas*	9:42
6.	*Miserere*	3:00
7.	*Jesu*	7:32
8.	*Bogi turrada*	5:22
9.	*Corsicana* and *canto in re*	3:31
10.	*Canto in re*	4:20
11.	*Gara poetica*	3:07
12.	*Ballu all'organetto*	4:40

SARDINIAN BALLADS

1. ***A tenore* song.** *Boghe'e notte,* followed by *ballu torrau* (dance song). Sung by singers from Fonni: Francesco Mulas, *bassu;* Francesco "Roma" Mureddu, *contra;* Francesco "Baralla" Mureddu, *boghe;* Giovanni "Corceddu," *mesa boghe.*
   REFERENCE: chapter 4, "Orgosolo."
   Recorded at the home of Cristoforo Bottaru in August 1993.
   TEXT: *ottava;* message sent via his daughter Maria to his friend Andrea who had emigrated to France.

> Since you are there, Maria,
> I wish to ask this favor of you:
> On behalf of Bottaru, Baralla, and the *"tenore"*
> Give our greetings to Andrea
> Tell him that in his village, which is also my own,
> He still has worthy friends.

We await his return to Fonni as soon as possible
To spend an hour with him.

2. *A tenore* song. *Ballu seriu* (dance song). *Tenores* of Bitti: Bachisio Pira, *bassu;* Tancredi Tucconi, *contra;* Piero Sanna, *boghe;* Mario de Melas, *mesa boghe.*
  REFERENCES: chapter 4, "Orgosolo," and chapter 8, "Irgoli."
  Recorded at the home of Piero Sanna, in his *cantina* (basement used primarily as a place to entertain guests), July 1993.

3. *A tenore* song. *Boghe'e notte antica.* Pinuccio Lai, *bassu;* Egidio Luche, *contra;* Tonino Obinu, *boghe;* Salvatore Lai, *mesa boghe.*
  REFERENCE: chapter 8, "Irgoli."
  Recorded with the assistance of Pribislav Pitoeff in a *cantina* in Irgoli, October 1989.
  TEXT: *ottava* of Giovanni Lai telling the "story" of the bridge of Irgoli-Onifai (only the first four verses are included on the disk).

To get around we need a bridge
For the one we have is old and in bad shape
They have deemed it unworkable
It was built before the 1930s . . .

4. *Ballu brincu.* (This selection, edited quite differently, appears on recording #1 listed under "Recordings and Films" in the bibliography of *Sardinian Chronicles*). Jew's harp: Salvatore Lai; Guitar: Salvatore Vacca. Singers: Emanuele Chessa and Salvatore Vacca.
  REFERENCE: chapter 8, "Irgoli."
  Recorded in the Vacca bar in Irgoli, August 1979.
  A satirical text.

Black eyes and curly hair
Even her chatter is pleasant
And the blouse she wears is fresh rose
It seems embroidered by a nun. . .
Who has no wife sleeps alone
And spends his life uncomforted
When he seeks a wife and doesn't find one
He ties knots in his sheets.

5. *Launeddas. Ballu* performed on a *Fiorassiu* (one of the types of instruments belonging to the *launeddas* family).
  REFERENCE: chapter 6, "Jerzu."

Recorded in Paris in the Department of Ethnomusicology of the Musée de l'Homme with the assistance of Jean Schwarz, February 1981.

6. *Miserere* of Holy Week. (This selection, edited quite differently, appears on recording #6 listed under "Recordings and Films" in the bibliography of *Sardinian Chronicles*). Singers of the *concurdu 'e su Rosariu* of Santu Lussurgiu: Giovanni Ardu, *bassu;* Mario Corona, *contra;* Antonio Migheli, *boghe;* Roberto Irriu, *contralto.*
REFERENCE: chapter 9, "Santu Lussurgiu."
Recorded in Santu Lussurgiu during the procession of Holy Thursday, 1985.
TEXT: Psalm 50.

7. *Jesu* of Holy Week. Singers of the Oratorio di Santa Croce Castelsardo: Angelo Garruccio, *bassu;* Matteo Santoni, *contra;* Giovanni Pintus, *bogi;* Salvatore Brozzu, *falzittu.*
REFERENCE: chapter 10, "Castelsardo."
Recorded in February 1991 in Paris at a concert commemorating the death of a friend, Aldo Vitale.
Liturgical text of oral tradition.

8. *Bogi turrada* of Aggius performed by singers from Castelsardo: Salvatore Tica, *bogi;* Matteo Santoni, *contra;* Giuseppe Brozzu, *falsittu.*
Reference to the traditional song of Aggius and its avatars: chapter 11, "Aggius."
Recorded in Castelsardo, around a table at Giuseppe Brozzu's, November 1992.

All these caresses and all this friendship are of no use to me:
If you are not here, my heart and my mind will never be at rest,
My heart cannot rest if I don't see you, delicate flower
I love you so much that I could be at your side at any moment.

9. *Corsicana,* followed immediately by *canto in re.* Guitar song performed as a serenade. Singers and guitarist from Siligo.
REFERENCE: chapter 7, "Thiesi."
Recorded with the assistance of Pribislav Pitoeff in Siligo during a serenade, October 1989.

10. *Canto in re.* Guitar song performed by professional singers. Singers: Franco De Nani, Francesco Falchi, Francesco De Muro; guitar: Bruno Malutrottu; accordion: Claudio De Sena.
REFERENCE: chapter 6, "Thiesi."

Recorded with the assistance of Severino Carboni, at the patron saint fête of Galtelli, August 1992.

11. *Gara poetica* (poetry joust). The poets are Antonio Piredda and Salvatore Budroni. Chorus: shepherds from Desulo.
REFERENCE to the art of poets: chapter 1, "The Ferry."
Recorded during the fête of San Basilio, Desulo, 1979.
The themes debated are "art" and "nature."

Piredda ("art"):
Oh, esteemed colleague, calm yourself
Now listen to my answer <
All kinds of sheep,
I take them and shear them closely <
I curdle the milk in the milk cart
And when it is curdled, I make cheese <
You can see that I use it like an expert
But you are unable to do so<>

Budroni ("nature"):
So, in your opinion, I'm of little worth <
And you say as much to everyone <
But you do not put yourself out to make an effort <
For it is I who awaken you and it is I who put you to sleep <
And to make cheese, you need curds <
This you cannot deny <
Why then do you brag and swagger <
For without me you would be unable to curdle it <>

Piredda ("art"):
Allow me to continue fairly,
Oh, Budroni, do not talk so arrogantly <
You have informed me that you could
Put a person to sleep or wake them up <
If someone is unable to fall asleep,
I can simply offer a sleeping pill <
Let me give you one now,
And if I wish, you will sleep for a long time <>

< signals the chorus's intervention
<> signals the final chorus's intervention

12. ***Ballu all'organetto.*** Dance played on the diatonic accordion. Suite performed for the *ballu in piazza* (dance held in the village square) by Salvatore Chessa of Irgoli.

REFERENCES: chapter 2, "Desulo"; chapter 3, "Oliena"; chapter 4, "Orgosolo"; chapter 8, "Irgoli."

Recorded with the assistance of Pribislav Pitoeff during the "long fête" of San Serafino in Ghilarza, 1989.

INDEX

Index